4/13/13

To Isabel,

May you &
your knowledge and
wisdom with others ok
your journey.

With love,
Linda B. Howard[?]

# I CAN RELATE TO THAT!

## A TOOLBOX FOR LIFE'S JOURNEY

*Linda Burd Howard, Ph.D.*

authorHOUSE®

*AuthorHouse™*
*1663 Liberty Drive*
*Bloomington, IN 47403*
*www.authorhouse.com*
*Phone: 1-800-839-8640*

*Published by AuthorHouse   11/14/2012*

*ISBN: 978-1-4772-4113-4 (sc)*
*SIBN: 978-1-4772-4114-1 (hc)*
*ISBN: 978-1-4772-4112-7 (e)*

*Library of Congress Control Number: 2012912635*

# Contents

# Preface:
# Finding Yourself

About twelve years ago I went to a psychologist. I needed some relationship guidance as I was uncertain about the kind of romantic relationship I wanted, or if in fact, I really wanted one. Towards the end of our first session the psychologist said, "Clearly you don't want to go from relationship to relationship for the rest of your life."

But that wasn't clear to me at all. Had she been listening? If she had, she'd have known that I actually enjoyed serial monogamy. Each time I experienced a new relationship I learned about myself, saw the world through the eyes of an interesting person and led a lifestyle different from the previous one. I found it all exciting, and since my children were increasingly busy with their own activities and lives, I saw no downside. Apparently, the psychologist didn't relate to my feelings or experiences and drew her own conclusion; a conclusion to which she'd have come, even without knowing my history or my feelings; my presence didn't seem to matter either, as her prejudices were in place well before I entered the room. I never returned.

I began thinking of all the people who had come to see me professionally. About half to three-quarters of the clients with whom I've worked over the years had previously gone to other psychologists. Some had been in therapy with the same person for years but didn't feel they were making significant progress, while others had "tried" several psychologists or therapists, some for only a session, some for a few months. We all shared the same experience: these professionals didn't convey to their clients an understanding of their feelings, and often didn't seem to relate to their experiences at all. Moreover, there was a preconceived idea on the part of many of them about what their clients wanted or needed to be happy.

In my fifties it became obvious to me that my success rating with clients was due to my ability to relate to others' feelings. It wasn't that I had lived through exactly what my clients had experienced that made it possible for me to relate to them, it was that I had experienced the same feelings and thoughts in my own life, sometimes in similar situations, but frequently in very different ones. There was nothing that sounded "crazy" to me. Considering the circumstances of each person's life, what he or she felt seemed perfectly normal. I've often thought it paradoxical that perhaps one of the best qualifications for being a successful psychologist is surviving serious personal and/or family dysfunction. I wondered if the best psychological treatment was the care of the id by the odd!

If it's dysfunction you want, I'm your girl! From anorexia, bulimia, drug addiction, multiple divorces, clinical depression, anxiety, and the suicide attempts and hospitalizations of my children following the suicide of their father, my husband of fourteen years, I've survived it. I've survived two con-artist boyfriends, both of whom it turns out, were sociopaths. One of them stole the innocence and trust of my children, and both of them took a great deal of my time and money under false pretenses. The self-blame was devastating. Talk about guilt! How could I NOT have seen it? I'm a psychologist for God's sake! The one thing I knew for sure was that if ignorance is bliss I should have been a whole lot happier.

While I was still recovering from my husband's suicide my children tried to kill themselves several times. Richard left a note blaming me for his death, and my once adoring in-laws suddenly turned against all three of us. Both Jesse and Nikki thought they were to blame for their father's demise at his own hand, and their guilt was overwhelming. Like so many children who are left behind after the suicide of a parent, they thought if only they had been better, smarter, nicer, quieter, more athletic, etc., etc., the tragedy would never have happened. For quite a while they tried to punish themselves. My daughter didn't think she was entitled to any happiness, and often cut herself to take her mind off the emotional pain and the guilt, whereas my son acted out his anger and hurt by bringing misery upon himself and me. Each child was taken to hospitals by ambulances many times, and each was repeatedly sent to the psychiatric ward of a children's hospital. There were frequent calls from the police about Jesse's acting out, and I vividly recall leaving him at the County Psychiatric Hospital after Baker Acting him, thinking "What kind of mother does this?"

My life had become a nightmare. I didn't know who I was anymore. I had spent years creating the family I wanted, and now it was gone. I didn't know how to be a person whose husband had killed himself and whose two children were crazy. Jesse, my once sweet son, was now also a juvenile delinquent!

Who was I? What did I do to deserve this? What was I to do about my children's despair? How could I help them when I was so unstable? Was I in some way responsible for the unimaginable nightmare that had overtaken my family? How was I supposed to handle all of this by myself? Was everything I once believed about my marriage and my children a lie? I was lost. Really lost.

One evening, while driving home from visiting my daughter at the psychiatric ward, I got a call from the principal of my son's middle school. Jesse had been placed in a special class for children who needed constant supervision. After exerting much pressure on the Special Education Team that had placed Jesse in this restricted environment, he was finally allowed to leave the classroom on his own and have lunch with other children in the cafeteria. His teacher was not happy about cutting Jesse some slack, as he often criticized the rigid man for his inability to teach, his failure to know the answers to Jesse's questions, etc. My troubled but gifted son used his brilliant intellect to his disadvantage every chance he could.

As I was saying, while driving home from the hospital, Jesse's principal called to say Jesse came back from lunch late after he'd been caught kissing a girl and smoking on school property. When he returned to the classroom the teacher threatened to have Jesse expelled, whereupon he simply said, "Don't bother, I quit." He proceeded to walk out of the building, followed shortly thereafter by three police cars, one of which finally caught up with him and brought him back to school.

I didn't think I could take any more when I left the hospital that day, but when I hung up with the principal I found myself saying out loud, "Okay God, this is what you want me to have in my life? Well, bring it on. Give me everything you've got. I can take it. Bring it God, bring it."

Something incredible happened to me at that moment of complete surrender. I suddenly felt like I had the emotional fortitude to handle anything. Instantly, and I mean instantly, I stopped feeling the pain, exhaustion and guilt, and went on automatic pilot. From then on, I simply did whatever needed doing each day. I had been in so much pain that God blocked it somehow so I could survive.

I've read hundreds of self-help books in my life, but they didn't really help me. I was given instructions on how to change my behavior and was taught why changes were important for me to make. I gained the understanding that my actions and interactions were often self-defeating, and I understood the origins of the lousy choices I made. Despite all this, my behavior didn't change. When I became a psychologist and had a private practice, I knew I wasn't "supposed to" let clients know about my personal life. Yet whenever I shared a story from my life, the client remembered not only the story, but also the "lesson" linked to the story. Together they were effective in fostering change. After I finished writing this book, I took a course entitled *Healing Through Metaphors*, by Bill O'Hanlon. I realized that adding pictures as metaphors for the lessons would be of even greater help to the reader, as metaphors seem to reach the unconscious mind and further reinforce learning.

**I Can Relate To That!** is a compilation of what I've learned about finding my way to my True Self, and how I came to love myself and be joyful in spite of, or perhaps because of the pain I've endured. To this end, I have been completely honest and forthcoming about my feelings and experiences.

I've found much humor in our universal experiences of worry, uncertainty and fear. It's because we're all so similar that the comedy and disclosures of people like Chris Rock and Robin Williams are so hysterically funny. We relate to their trials, tribulations and observations. There's no denying it: we are funny, so humor dots the landscape of our journey.

What qualifies me to write a self-help book is that I've learned how to be, not just fine, but really happy with myself, and to find joy in every day. As far as giving advice goes, I lack only one qualification: I'm not a hairdresser!

**I Can Relate To That!** is organized according to the themes that have had the greatest impact on my clients and me. Like you (probably), I went into the world without the gear or tools needed for a life journey, so I've assembled a life skills toolbox to assist you on yours. The tools I give you for each lesson appear at the tops of the pages. While some of the tools are mental pictures, some are literal. As you read the lessons, visualize how the tools might be used and imagine their applications in each of the experiences on the opposite or following pages. The tools will then automatically come to mind in circumstances in which they'll be helpful to you, and your mind will jump to the experiences and lessons with which they're associated in the book. Thanks to neuroscience the connections occur naturally. I know you'll identify with many of my experiences and most of my feelings. That identification will stamp in the lessons.

In Part One, *On Your Journey*, you'll see how much you have in common with the other travelers. As for how well you'll do on this trip, you can't get it wrong, but you can get it painfully. That's what we're here to avoid. You'll find out why you need to identify your issues and you'll get the tools to help you do so.

You'll learn how the Universe speaks to you without words, yet you can still "hear" its wisdom. Translating Universe-speak is made easy on the first leg of your journey.

I'm sure you've noticed many red flags in your life, but my guess is you didn't see them until you looked in your rear-view mirror. Part One will assist you in seeing those flags before you pass them by without noticing them. You'll learn why it's important to pay attention to them, and when you learn the language of the Universe you can avoid most red flags once and for all. Even if you experience "failure" at some point on your journey, you'll come to appreciate the benefits of gaining a new perspective on that word.

There will be people with some serious attitudes on your journey. Some of them might even have, OMG, PMS! Nasty? You think? No problem. Just take a pen and some paper with you as you set out, so when you're angry you can express yourself by writing instead of fighting. When you learn what your issues are, you might realize you're not really angry about what you think you're angry about, but rather, something that happened long ago but is still interfering with your serenity. (Like you've ever been serene, right?)

When you change your focus from anger to gratitude you'll begin to experience life differently, and you'll noticeably accelerate your growth. You'll be one giant step closer to finding your True Self and experiencing the insights and joys of that discovery.

On the second leg of our trip, *On Responsibility*, you'll find out who's responsible for what happens on this journey. You may be very surprised. Armed with new understanding, you might start to make assumptions about people in your life, but you'll relate to the experience that exemplifies why that's not a good idea.

You'll have to park your ego at the side of the road in order to learn a few things in this section; you could be tripping over it without even knowing it. Oh, and BTW, you'll want to rid yourself of some of your old gear; it's weighing you down big time. If you have trouble letting go of things this could be challenging, even if you only have to toss out a few words. You can spare just four even if you're a hoarder, can't you? Your entire life will change for the better, but you've got to get rid of those four crippling words.

Now that you're getting much closer to your goal, guess what? It's time to change course! Clearly, this whole journey is a metaphor for life, and if changing course when you've been working hard to get to a goal isn't exactly like what happens in life, my name is Tina Turner. (When I was a kid, my brother used to tell people our last name was Turner and my first name was Stomach.)

Assuming you've changed course, you may experience a sense of loss. You gals know how it is when a company stops manufacturing the one cosmetic you can't live without, right? It's kind of like that; you feel as though you have to start from the beginning. But this isn't a cosmetic; it's your life we're talking about here! Not that I wasn't seriously disturbed when Lancôme stopped making Photôgenic, mind you. Still, I wasn't what you'd call miserable. But I digress...

Changing course in life can create a sense of loss that may leave you feeling distraught. In fact, just about anything can leave you distraught if you let it, and if you've been miserable or depressed long enough you may just wonder if your particular kind of misery is "normal." You'll find out just how crazy or sane you are in Part Two.

Having changed course you might be somewhat lost, and maybe you're frustrated with the other travelers and ticked-off for reasons that aren't clear to you. It's not a good idea to act on your anger, so on the second leg of your journey you'll be given the tools to enable you to vent in a way that won't give you indigestion. One reason you might be angry is that you've loaned the others on the trip your jackets and sweaters and now you're getting cold and want them back. You're likely wondering why you didn't just say *no* when you were asked to lend them. Learning to say *no* is on the responsibility path, too.

Now that we're on the third part of our trip, *On Control*, you may already be feeling as though your life is under control. After all, you've come pretty far and have considered some ideas you may never have thought about before. Get real!! Control is a biggie, so I guarantee if it's not an issue right now it will be again soon. Some people on your path may use silence as a way to control others. Can you relate? That's a strategy I'd advise you to avoid. I refuse to say another word about that now. Don't even think about it!

BTW, have you ever tried to make someone like you? When they finally want you, assuming they do, do you think you're in control then? What about trying to control how others act, what they say or how they feel? Control is tantamount to a gigantic chasm you have to cross in order to go any further on your path to happiness. If you don't learn to deal with it constructively you can easily destroy your relationships, to say nothing of impeding your whole life!

Just how much do you allow yourself to let go of control? Comfort Zone addresses that issue. Did you know there are methods you can use to train people to respond to you in certain ways? Teaching Others will show you how you've been training them all along, and will assist you in altering your training program if that's what you'd like to do. And you do have control over the choices you make, although usually, not every choice you'd like to be given is offered. Being a Mirror is just one technique you can use to affect how others treat you, while Giving Advice to people in an attempt to get them to do what you'd like them to do may just backfire. Doing more of what didn't work before won't work either, but you sure can waste a lot of time and energy that way. Take my advice, read all about it in Part Three!

Finally, let's go down the love trail, my personal favorite, which is Part Four, *On Love*. There are some facts you should know before you decide whether or not you want to take the rest of your journey with a particular someone. If you don't know the facts you could be confused about whether you want your "Plus One" to be a significant other or just another who isn't very significant at all. Maybe you think you'd rather be an *I* than a *We*. Either way, this is one place on your journey you'll want to look back and find some clues to how you can successfully move forward. You'll learn why it's crucial to put yourself first when it comes to love. I've collected some great tools for you to use when the road gets bumpy on the love trail.

And who acts more "crazy" than someone in love? What is it about love that makes us so stupid, so gullible, so willing to overlook everything from bad hygiene to criminal behavior? The focus on these hills and valleys is REALITY. Blech!

There are ways to bond with someone that are simple and cheap (I'm trying hard to abstain from the obvious joke in this context). The chapters entitled Bonding Made Easy and The Ratio give you a leg up, shall we say, on creating and sustaining love. Internet dating is all about what NOT to do on your favorite site when looking for a mate. According to ninety-five percent of people to whom I've spoken, good advice in this area is much needed and should be taken very seriously. Finally, Stayin' Alive speaks to how you can best honor those who've passed, and explains how you can connect with their spirits, while Creating Good Memories explains the importance of moving from mourning to joy after a loss, and shows you how to introduce friends and loved ones who are living now to those who have transitioned.

This is just a little metaphoric snapshot of our journey. If you're tired already, why not sit down, relax, and read a good book?

# Part One:

# On Your Journey

Absolutely essential tools to have in your toolbox
when you start your journey:

1.  **BINOCULARS:**  to enable you to look back into your past

    **MAGNIFYING GLASS:**  to see your issues clearly

2.  **AMPLIFIER:**  to listen to the Universe

3.  **BINOCULARS:**  to see red flags from a distance

4. **TODAY ON A CALENDAR:** to remind you to constantly practice living in the NOW

5. **ERASER:** to eliminate the word failure from your vocabulary

6. **PEN AND PAPER:** to express your feelings safely

7. **SODIUM PENTATHOL** (Truth Serum): to be honest with yourself

8. **TIMER:** to remind you it's time to express gratitude

# Got Issues?

In psychology, an *issue* is considered anything from the past that gets in the way of your life being joyful and in the moment. It always seems like the other guy or something outside yourself is "making you" feel some way or do something, and it never feels like it's your fault. Wherever you find relationships of any kind you'll find issues. Some issues can prevent you from leaving your house or making contact with anyone, but even isolation from others won't obliterate your issues.

With this in mind, I ask you fellow traveler, do you have issues?

HELLO! Does a wild bear poop in the woods?

Sometimes people refer to issues as baggage, but the results are the same. The questions to ask yourself are: Can I identify at least three (an arbitrary number) of my issues? What caused them to be my issues? How do they interfere with my functioning well? Only when you know how to determine if something is an issue for you can you reduce or eliminate the problems caused by those awful little buggers.

The more issues you have, the less your chances of happiness, because issues come up constantly and sabotage you, making you feel left out, slighted, cheap, stupid, lazy, fat, ugly, different, etc. When you isolate issues that originated in your PAST, and separate them from your PERCEPTION of the PRESENT, you can truly become joyful, not just okay. So whether you have one or one hundred issues or a pound or a ton of baggage, you can increase your happiness by facing your issues honestly, understanding their origin, identifying their effects on your life TODAY, and making the DECISION to change your reactions to the circumstances in which they're activated.

Some clues for you to watch for while scurrying around looking for your issues may be helpful. Do you find yourself disappointed or unhappy in relationships but feel as though you can't understand or control what's causing your unhappiness? Do you frequently argue with loved ones over trivial matters? Are you often accused of being defensive, angry, or overreacting? Do you make the same poor choices over and over again? It's not one trigger in particular that signals an issue; it's the PATTERN of behaviors you can see when you honestly examine yourself and your relationships. The binoculars in your toolbox are there because only by looking back at your past can you see that certain behaviors and/or events have affected the formation of your patterns. Understanding this enables you to own the issues that are yours and take responsibility for either changing your reactions or recognizing your role in the challenges you face.

Sometimes, even when we know all this, it's still difficult to tell if the problems we face originate from our issues or someone else's. This is where the magnifying glass from your toolbox comes in. It makes everything more distinct and therefore, easier to ferret out.

The challenge is to be aware of the patterns and identify the thoughts, feelings and behaviors OF YOURS that keep creating problems in your life. Then you have to make a conscious DECISION to change; that's where your INTENTION to deal with your issues comes in. Finally, putting your intentions into ACTIONS will enable you to take responsibility for your part in every issue. As we all know from experience, we can't change anyone else's behavior, but we can change our own. I disagree with those psychologists who suggest that looking back is more detrimental than helpful; it's necessary to look back, but it is certainly detrimental to stare.

Put on your running shoes if you're attracted to someone who denies having any issues. And remember that no issue is so small it can't be blown way out of proportion. In fact, that's sometimes the nature of issues.

It's too bad we can't swap the problems caused by our issues. After all, everyone knows how to solve the other person's.

# Got Issues?

*my experience*

Until relatively late in life, I had more issues than *The National Enquirer*. As a little kid, mine was one of the only two Jewish families for miles, or at least that's how it seemed. All the little girls in the neighborhood had various shades of blonde or red hair, which shockingly, grew only out of their heads! Mine, however, was pitch black and grew all over, as though Martha Stewart fertilized me regularly. It was everywhere; on my arms, covering my legs, creating a unibrow of epic proportions and even a moustache to rival that of Groucho Marx. I associated blonde with pretty, delicate and feminine. I associated myself with Zippy the chimp. I can recall feeling masculine and wishing I could be slight of build, blonde and a lover of liverwurst with mayo on white bread. I always felt left out and that I didn't belong anywhere.

The other kids' families did stuff together. From my house I could frequently hear laughter and loud talking originating from the back porches of homes on our block at which many parents of the kids in the neighborhood gathered to play poker. On those occasions the smell of beer wafted through the little community. Not only did I feel as though I didn't belong, I felt my parents were outsiders too. They didn't participate in those gatherings. They neither played poker nor drank beer. They didn't even talk loud. The only life in our backyard was that of a stray snapper turtle residing in a little wading pool. I had more in common with the turtle than with the other kids. We were both alone with nowhere to go, we were both ugly, and neither of us played poker! Nobody at my house fit in.

When I was in the fifth grade my family moved to a predominantly Jewish community where I aspired with all my heart to being a JAP (Jewish American Princess), to no avail. There must have been a committee in the town to keep America's kids beautiful, and it had apparently passed a law banning the infamous unibrow, for there wasn't a single one (pun intended) in sight. My parents refused to be on the committee, and in fact, had nothing but disdain for its members, all of whom rigidly enforced its rules. Frequent "beauty parlor" visits were mandatory, even for the Mickey Mouse Club set.

I was not just the new kid; I was the new, hairy kid. I'm pretty sure I was the only girl in my grade who never went to Disneyland, never shopped at Saks with my mom, never had my hair done professionally and wasn't allowed to wear "nylons" (stockings). I didn't have long chiffon scarves in the fifth grade either, but all the popular girls wore them, especially on the days we had "Social Dancing." They also wore "training bras," which I guess were supposed to somehow train one's barely there breasts to develop into perky little appendages that required the next bra step up: the coveted AA. It didn't matter to me that the girls had fewer curves than the chalkboard. All I knew was bra straps were visible under their clothes but not under mine. I wanted to fit in so much that I cut off the bottom of one of my grandmother's old slips and wore the upper part under my clothes so I could be like the other girls. If I couldn't actually have a bra, at least people might think I did if they detected the straps beneath my blouses.

The day finally came when my mother allowed me to wear nylons. Have you ever seen stockings on a chimpanzee? It isn't pretty. The stockings over which I'd waged war with my mother turned out to be, not a right of passage, but rather, a cringe benefit of my mother's permission and a statement of my inability to fit in, regardless of what I did. There was always a caveat to what my mother allowed me to do; I could wear nylons but couldn't shave my legs. Think sheer stockings over a fully-grown Chiapet. I clearly remember the girls standing in a circle of starched blouses (only "permanent press" at my house), straight skirts and chiffon scarves, turning to look at me and laugh.

Regardless of the accomplishments I've had over the years, the love of friends and the acceptance of esteemed people, I've never completely gotten over the feeling of being an outsider. To this day, when I walk into a room where there's a group of women, if one of them happens to look at me while laughing I get a pang of anxiety. Neither rational thought, popularity, nor the attention and accolades of others has ever entirely changed the left out feelings that grew out of my childhood experiences.

That's why the very first item I put in my toolbox was binoculars. They enable me to see way back into the past, so I can observe my patterns of behavior over time. Then I take out my magnifying glass and enlarge the similarities that exist in different situations from the past to see where my emotional reactions were similar. It's usually the events that were previously traumatic to me that cause me to be upset in present situations, even though the situations that upset me now may have only the smallest of similarities to those that were originally traumatic. The awareness that the events that originally generated these painful emotions are in the PAST helps me successfully deal with these feelings. However, sometimes the feelings themselves still get attached to very DIFFERENT events in the PRESENT because of one or more emotional associations my brain makes from the past event to the present event. It's like I'm experiencing all the emotions from long ago again, only this time they're not attached to events that would now, by themselves, cause such strong emotions.

It's also important to know that hurtful past experiences that get attached to today's upsets usually feel as though someone's behavior or something that happened MADE YOU feel or act a certain way. You can use your magnifying glass here to examine the evidence more closely. Look carefully at the actual behaviors that took place recently. For example: 1. *Joe entered the store.* (NOT: Joe *pushed* his way into the store.) 2. *Sam, the store manager, looked up from his book.* (NOT: Sam, the store manager, looked up from his book *angrily.*) 3. *Sam told Joe not to walk to the back of the store.* (NOT: Sam *bullied* Joe into staying away from the back of the store.) Don't add any modifiers like adjectives or adverbs, and don't add your feelings or anyone else's presumed feelings; just the facts. Does your reaction to the FACTS make sense? Does it make sense considering what your issues are? If the answer to the first question is no, but the answer to the second is yes, you'll know it's YOUR issues that are getting in the way because they're creating a perception of the experience that's based on your past, not your present. If they are, it's up to you to separate the old feelings from the present situation.

Today when my reactions are over-reactions, I always take the major tools out of my toolbox. If it weren't for my binoculars and magnifying glass, I'd never know that when things seem much bigger than they actually are, I'm reacting to more than the person or situation in front of me. That's when I remind myself that feelings aren't facts.

And that, my friend, is the nitty-gritty of an issue.

# Listening to the Universe

Have you ever heard the Universe talking to you? It talks to us constantly, but since the Universe can't speak our language, we have to learn the language in which it speaks to us.

Here are some examples of Universe-speak from my list of personal favorites:

- Ever get into trouble for gossiping? The Universe is telling you not to gossip.
- Ever have to rush so much in the morning that you get off to a bad start? The Universe is saying *Set your alarm earlier.*
- Ever feel like a doormat because you keep choosing friends who don't reciprocate when you go out of your way for them? The Universe is letting you know you should find different friends.
- Ever feel exhausted because you're allowing your kids or your commitments to run you ragged? That's the Universe's way of telling you to schedule less and rest more.

If you don't feel like a winner you may need to turn up the amps and listen more carefully. In order to stop making the same mistakes over and over again you have to hear what the Universe is telling you. Then take a few deep breaths, sit quietly and get in touch with what you've been feeling lately. Pay very close attention to your life and what you're being "told" by events, circumstances and outcomes.

Psychologists do something very similar. We listen to your feelings and help you interpret what the Universe is trying to tell you. Then we give you choices about how to change your life and explore whether change is what you want. Once you learn the "language" of the Universe, you can explore by yourself.

It's uncomfortable to listen to someone who's saying what we don't want to hear, and it can be even more challenging to accept that the Universe is telling us to make difficult changes, but the Universe never lies.

Being alive is like being at an auction. Before we're about to lose a coveted item, like our good health, for example, the Universe picks up the gavel and screams, "Fair Warning!" Unless we act quickly, we can lose it all.

# Listening To The Universe
*my experience*

You're probably going to think the first example I'm going to give you is gross and disgusting, but I'm going to tell you anyway because the experience struck me as a great example of listening to the Universe.

This morning my toilet started to clog. You know how sometimes after you flush, the water starts to rise and any minute there's going to be a catastrophe? That's what happened this morning.

I always keep a pair of rubber scrubbing gloves in the bathroom cabinet. There are only a couple of seconds before the water flows over the top, right? Well, for one of them, I stood there debating if I should get the rubber gloves and stick my gloved hand in the toilet to unclog it, or if I should start gathering building materials for the ark I was about to need. I went for it! Hoping the water wasn't higher than the top of my glove, I stuck my hand into the bowl and unclogged it!

The water went down immediately, and I realized the Universe had just spoken to me. It said, "Honey, when you see a potential problem, don't wait. Get in there, no matter how unpleasant it may seem. Take action before it's too late so you can prevent an even bigger problem."

Later this morning, while in a rush, I was trying to open a small plastic bag filled with tiny beads. I impatiently tugged too hard, the bag broke, and beads went all over the floor. The Universe was saying, "Slow down. Rushing will cost you time and energy." I've been hearing that message from the Universe for years. Evidently, I need quite a bit of reminding, so the Universe keeps giving me opportunities to demonstrate that I've finally learned the lesson. Apparently, I haven't.

I knew a man who was so lazy he ate little packaged fruit pies for dinner because they didn't require much cooking. It wasn't long before the Universe spoke to him through his doctor.

When the Universe seeks to tell you you're down to nothing, rest assured, God is up to something.

# Red Flags

How many times have you been shockingly disappointed by someone's behavior, only to realize later that there were clues you should have noticed all along; clues that would have alerted you to potential disaster had you only paid attention to them. Get out those binoculars again. You're going to look way into the future as well as back in the past this time. Red flags are all about the dangers that lie ahead, so you'll be looking back to see patterns from the past that can affect events in the future.

For example, if someone frequently puts other people down, what does this tell you? He or she has a need to devalue others. Happy people don't do that. Why is it important to notice whether this is a pattern in someone's behavior or just an offhanded slight? If the person has a PATTERN of devaluing others, you will most likely be a target. Notice when someone talks behind the backs of their so-called friends, because they'll talk behind your back too.

If someone lashes out on a regular basis at drivers, service people like waitresses and store clerks, or at his or her own children, this is the pattern of a bully. If you see the red flag of a bully and CHOOSE to have a relationship with such a person, don't be surprised when the next rumor or hissy fit is directed towards you.

If a person is a blamer and never takes responsibility for anything that goes wrong in life, you'll be blamed for some mishap; it's just a matter of time. Sometimes we're bowled over by the patterns of behavior that were right in front of us all along but we just didn't want to notice, although in retrospect, they were as obvious as a cactus in a handful of feathers.

For example, if each time you go to the doctor the office plants are dead, that's a red flag.

# Red Flags
*my experience*


My life has been strewn with red flags. Frequently, those of us who love drama choose to go towards those flags instead of steering clear of them. After all, they're RED!

Creative people like artists and writers seem to be more vulnerable to the lure of red flags waved by those with outrageous stories. I've frequently described as "interesting," people who share facts about their lives that others find entirely implausible. In the past, what my more grounded friends readily saw as trouble markers, I excused based on my willingness to believe that people were who they said they were. While others recognize a snake salesman and run, I'm apt to be drawn to those beautiful snakes.

For over a year, a man who claimed to be a roofer and a contractor lived with me. I fell for him shortly after he started working in my home about a year after Richard's death. He was supposed to be doing renovation projects, although nothing was ever completed. I gave him paycheck after paycheck but saw no results, all the while believing his stories about the necessary preparations he was making by constantly going out to get tools, compare prices or meet with subcontractors to collaborate on the best ways to do this or repair that. Every week I gave him more cash with which to buy supplies needed for starting new projects. However, after fifty-two weeks nothing had yet been completed.

Now, using my binoculars, of course I can see countless times I was fooled. One day I told him he had to finish everything he'd started before I'd give him another penny. It was the night before I was to undergo minor surgery, and the doctor had given me a sedative so I could sleep. Just as I was dozing off, this con artist put one of my checks, made payable to him, in front of me to sign. After the operation I didn't remember signing the check. The following week I got a call from my bank asking me about a signature on a check that was very different from my usual one. Sure enough, when I saw the check it all came back to me. The man had been scamming money from me all along but I didn't want to believe it so I paid no attention to my uneasy feelings, which were the Universe's way of telling me something wasn't right. Red flags are to the Universe what punctuation is to writing. They're helpers in the bigger picture, and they're vital to our understanding of the whole.

I still have difficulty seeing red flags sometimes. I've asked my good friends to let me know if they see any red banners flying around me, and to tell me when they do. You have to ask for assistance in life when you need it. Now that I've done that, I take everything they say to heart, and sometimes when those flags are held up to me I can see them as trouble markers instead of colorful enticements along my path.

Red flags are there to remind us to pay attention to our lives. They're the Universe's way of saying "Caution!" Use your binoculars to look both in back of you and ahead of you so you can better forsee that if you do what you always did, you'll get what you always got. For instance, if you're looking for an electrician and find one who's been nicknamed Sparky, send him packing. That's a red flag.

Recently I spotted a red flag entirely on my own. I'm getting really good at this! I wanted someone to help me clean my house, so I set up interviews with several housekeepers. When the first one showed up carrying a magazine called *Good Enough Housekeeping,* I crossed her right off my list!

# Worrying

Think about the very last problem that freaked you out. You know, the thing you worried about, had anxiety over and thought would ruin your life. Consider what a wreck you were, how completely overtaken you were by "what ifs," and how much energy you expended worrying.

Did worrying help you in any way? Did it make the outcome better? Was the worrying really worth all you put yourself, and probably everyone else through, or did the problem work itself out? Did your freak out have any positive effect at all? Even if your worst fears were realized, you got past it and now you're okay, right?

How many times in your life have you gone through that little scenario with different problems? Maybe seven or eight—THOUSAND times? If you can relate to that (and I know you can because I have astounding psychic abilities), get your day-on-a-page calendar out of your toolbox and find today, because you have to live in it to be a happy camper.

When we are in the NOW moment, experiencing nothing else but exactly what is going on around us moment by moment, we are free of worry.

Life works itself out exactly as it's supposed to, which doesn't mean it works out exactly as you'd like it to. Your worrying has absolutely no effect whatsoever on life's outcomes. It does, however, make you miserable, and the effects of chronic elevations of the "stress hormone" cortisol include elevated blood sugar and blood pressure, increased fat accumulation, difficulty concentrating and remembering, and even WRINKLES!!!! OMG!

Most of the time, the awful result you fear doesn't happen, and if it does, it's happening because there's a lesson you're supposed to learn from it. You're supposed to figure out what the Universe is trying to tell you.

Did you lose the job because you weren't sufficiently prepared? Did the girl reject you because you're wimpy? Did you fail the test because you didn't study hard enough? Did you ignore your gut feeling that something was wrong, only to find out later that the guy who claimed to be a CEO (Chief Executive Officer) was actually an ODT (Olympic Drug Tester)? Learn the lesson and forget the worrying. If you can't help worrying, at least remember that worrying can't help you either.

# Worrying
*my experience*

I was the proverbial worrywart back in my twenties and thirties. Even when I was having fun, there was a little worrying voice inside my head, chattering away. I was worried about how I looked, if I was thin enough, how others perceived me, if I offended anyone, what people thought about what I said, blah, blah, blah, blah. The worry was never-ending, and it zapped nearly all my energy. I was exhausted most of the time and came to rely on amphetamines and cocaine to get me through each day.

If we are truly in the NOW we aren't worried. After all, worry is about something that's already happened (past) or something that might happen (future). If we stay in the present we don't worry. I added a day-on-a-page calendar to my toolbox as soon as I realized this. It's made a huge positive impact on my life.

The first time I made a decision to practice living in the moment I was taking a walk to get some exercise. It was as if I was seeing the colors of the trees, the flowers and the sky for the first time. I kept drifting back to worries and had to repeatedly remind myself, "Come back, Linda," pulling myself back into the moment. When I was in the NOW, every detail in nature jumped out at me. Spiders were spinning stunning webs, lizards were running under rocks, bees were circling flowers. I FELT the energy of all the life around me; the grass was growing, old flowers were dying and new ones blooming, clouds were moving and the breeze was blowing through the trees. I felt part of life rather than apart from it, as I'd previously felt when I was walking and worrying, worrying, worrying.

As I practiced pulling myself back into the NOW in my daily life, the worry thoughts decreased and the EXPERIENCES increased. Everything became intensified because I was fully present. The length of time between NOW and mind-drifting into the worry mode became longer as I practiced. I'm not expecting to receive my guru degree in the mail anytime soon, however; in any given hour I may still have to pull myself back fifty times. Remember: progress, not perfection.

I knew I'd come a long way in overcoming my usual low-grade worrying when I drove my new convertible to a shopping center and left the top down while I went into a store. I began trying on clothes, joking and talking with the salespeople. When I came out of the dressing room it was pouring outside. I quickly ran out of the store with my purchases, trying to dodge the raindrops, when I saw my brand new convertible collecting water. I'd completely forgotten that my top was down. Up until then I thought the trouble with bucket seats was that not everybody has the same size bucket, but now my bucket seats actually were buckets! I pulled myself into the NOW where worry doesn't exist and I realized I was smiling. I noticed how the rain felt on my cheeks and what fun it was to run in the puddles. I got into the car, put the top up and looked at the back seats, which were filled with water. On the six minute ride home I must have pulled myself back into the moment at least fifteen times. But while I was in the moment without worrying, I actually enjoyed the experience of driving while dripping wet.

When in the NOW, NO THOUGHTS exist to detract from the experience. I didn't feel guilty or stupid for leaving the top down. Because my thoughts had stopped, so did the feelings those thoughts usually activate. As soon as I got home I wiped the car down, got all the water out and let the car run with the heat on for about ten minutes. No damage was done and it was actually fun!

A catchy, clever line from a Twelve-Step Program will help you remember all this:

Yesterday's history, tomorrow's a mystery and today is a gift; that's why they call it the present.

# Failure Has a Bad Rap

Failure has gotten a bad rap. It's really another name for learning, and it's the most frequently traveled highway to success. How else do we learn and grow?

Sure it's people's successes that we see, but what we don't see is how much failure they experienced on their journeys and how much determination was needed to achieve success. Failure is just giving up before you succeed. If you give up you'll never know if success was waiting for you at the next crossroad.

Most successful people have long lists of failures and rejections behind them. In fact, it's been said that the only difference between a failure and a success is the tenacious pursuit of a goal. What makes for success is that very same relentlessness that drives you crazy when your children don't stop nagging until they get what they want. It's good to remember this when the nagging becomes so annoying the only thing that keeps you going is their threat of leaving home!

Believe me, there's no greater driving ambition than that of a seventeen-year-old boy who wants a car and refuses to fail at getting one. Think of the nagging as tenacity, and regard it as a quality that will be helpful to him in the long run. Still, mothers of teenagers know why some animals eat their young.

General George Patton, arguably one of the greatest generals of all time said, "Success is how high you bounce after you reach bottom." Robert F. Kennedy assured us that, "Only those who dare to fail greatly dare to achieve greatly." To paraphrase hundreds of successful people, if you haven't failed you haven't aimed high enough. So take out the toolbox, pull out your eraser, and eliminate that nasty F word forever!

Success is a personal standard. To me success is overcoming obstacles you thought you were incapable of overcoming, and you only thought you couldn't overcome them because you "failed" at so much so often that you either believe it's hopeless for you to keep trying, or you're afraid to fail again. In other words, the really impressive part of succeeding is having the courage, strength and determination to remain committed to something despite constantly running into walls.

So if you have a talent or a great idea, be like a postage stamp and stick to it until you get where you want to be.

Ultimately, success is getting what you want, and happiness is wanting what you get.

Remember this: wisdom comes from mistakes. You gain KNOWLEDGE when you read the fine print...you gain WISDOM from the mistakes you make when you don't!

# Failure Has a Bad Rap

*my experience*

When I was getting sober in New York City, I went to Twelve-Step meetings constantly. I learned that I had to change just about every attitude and behavior in my repertoire. I DECIDED to take up an activity that was completely different from anything I'd done in the past. I thought I'd try painting on inexpensive T-shirts, which was less of a commitment than painting on canvas.

I bought acrylic paints, brushes, and a dozen white T-shirts. I could hardly wait to start. Opening the plastic bags filled with the stuff of real artists gave me a jolt of adrenalin. I was ready to dig in, except for the fact that I wasn't able to put paint on a shirt. I stood there with shiny green paint on my new brush, but literally could not make a single stroke on the shirt. What the ...?

At first I had no idea what to make of my sudden, very specific paralysis. I washed the green paint from the brush and decided to try pink. I'd make a flower. How difficult could that be?

Again, nothing.

I sat down to figure out what was going on, and it didn't take but a moment for me to realize how terrified I was of making a mistake. I thought, *So what? Nobody has to see the shirt! Besides, I have eleven others!* I got up and forced myself to make a stroke. I didn't like the imperfect line I'd made and decided I just couldn't paint.

*What a stupid idea, painting T-shirts! I haven't picked up a paintbrush since I was a kid, and I stunk then!* I continued to berate myself as I made some dinner. When I considered returning the twenty-seven items I'd purchased, I dreaded the thought of the cashier's reaction.

Here I was, a grown woman for heaven's sake, and I couldn't make two strokes with a paintbrush! The next morning I saw the evidence of my failure, starting my day off with a whimper instead of a bang. The painting experience kept gnawing at me. The art materials were all over the place and might as well have been a big sign blinking "LOSER." I didn't even want to touch them, so I left my apartment to go for a walk. When I reached the lobby, some little kids were there, just hanging out.

"Hey," I said, "how 'ya doing? You live in this building?"

Their mom, who had been talking to the doorman, came over to us. "Yes they do," she answered. Without thinking about it, I invited the three kids and their mother to paint shirts with me. I told the mom exactly why I needed their help. I simply explained that young children aren't afraid of making mistakes and I needed some good role models. She shook her head and smiled as if she could relate. She accepted my invitation.

When the four of them came up to my apartment the next evening the kids went right for the brushes and paints. Watching them paint with abandon was just what I needed. It was fabulous to witness their enjoyment of the PROCESS. My take on the experience completely changed. I realized THERE'S NO SUCH THING AS FAILURE IF YOU'RE HAVING FUN. Naturally, I put an eraser in my toolbox, and soon the word *failure* was ...poof! Gone.

When the group left with their wet shirts I painted a simple red rosebud with a long green stem and three leaves. I loved it and wore it proudly many times. More importantly, I no longer expected myself to "succeed." I just wanted to enjoy the experience of painting.

The Universe's message was powerful and clear.

The road to learning is paved with trials, not failures, and success is being happy wherever you are on that road RIGHT NOW.

# Write, Don't Fight

In my practice when clients are angry I advise them to write down what's bothering them before they approach the person at whom they're angry. I ask them to be very specific and stick to the point. Doing this helps organize thoughts and sort out feelings. It also gives a person time to chill out rather than lash out.

But here's the problem: now we have e-mail. That teensy-weensy little *send* button is easier to push than chocolate at recess. Push that button and your angry words are immortalized, to be resent to everyone you ever knew and those you've never even met. Each exclamation point and capitalized comment appears larger than life and can come back to haunt you. You've put your angry self in writing which can be used against you for eternity. To paraphrase Hemingway, the difference of one little word is the difference between lightning and lightning bug.

I'm still suggesting that you write your thoughts and feelings down in words, but not on that oh-so-easy to send and resend e-mail. That's why I've included some paper and a pen in your toolbox. Actually write on paper or create a Microsoft word document, but always wait twenty-four hours before deciding whether or not to send your letter.

As the old saying goes, the pen is mightier than the sword... and might I add, considerably easier to write with.

# Write, Don't Fight
*my experience*

Back in the day, there was a weekly series on T.V. called *The Mary Tyler Moore Show*. Mary was the *IT* girl. Everyone who watched her go through her trials and tribulations cheered her on, as show after show she continued to blossom.

One day when Mary was furious with her boyfriend, she vented to her close friend and co-worker, Murray. He suggested that Mary write her boyfriend a letter telling him everything she felt, what bothered her about him, and to explicitly state why she was so angry with him.

As usual, ever ready to take someone else's advice for the sake of self-betterment, Mary went home and wrote the letter. The next day she proudly strode into the office anticipating Murray's positive reaction to her completed assignment. Confidently, Mary handed it to her friend. As Murray read the letter he looked at Mary occasionally and said, "Good Mary, this is good." Mary simultaneously steamed and beamed.

After Murray read the letter he verbally applauded her. "Wow, Mary, this is just great. You've clearly spelled out why you're so mad, what he did, how you were affected by it...everything! Great job, Mary, it's perfect," he said.

Mary was thrilled by his response. As she licked the envelope into which she placed the letter, Murray jumped out of his chair and grabbed it from her. "Mary," he shouted, "the most important part is that you DON'T SEND the letter!"

While I don't make it a practice to use sitcoms as templates for living, I've made this an exception. Over the years I've written dozens of letters that are still in my filing cabinet under the heading *Unsent Letters.* Sometimes when I'm going through folders looking for something, I stumble upon a folder labeled *Letters to Linda.* The last time I read some of those letters I realized that the good memories I once had of the people who wrote them were obliterated by their everlasting angry words. When I read my own unsent angry letters now, I'm so grateful they didn't end up in someone else's filing cabinet! I don't ever want to be remembered for who I was at my very worst.

Thank you, Murray.

# Integrity

If you were to ask me to name the one thing that most affects a person's mental state, physical well-being and overall self-esteem, I'd have to say it's having personal integrity.

If you listen to the Universe, forget the word *failure*, and make a conscious DECISION to be who you really are, you'll be your authentic self and as such, you'll have integrity.

When you do or say things that aren't quite true just to be liked, please other people, or sound better than you think you are, you pay a price that's equal to your own happiness. Sure you might think you're appeasing someone for the time being, but on some level you'll feel bad about yourself for being less than honest. What's more, your immune system shuts down when you aren't true to yourself, so you're more susceptible to environmental toxins, clinical depression and even the common cold. One of the many functions that suffers is your ability to sleep peacefully, which reduces your body's energy to fight disease. The little bottle of liquid in your toolbox is Sodium Pentathol, better known as truth serum. It's time to get out that bottle.

The willingness to tell the truth, be who you are and say what you feel is enormously empowering. When you have integrity you're telling the world you're okay with yourself. Every time your actions don't come from integrity you're giving yourself the message that you're afraid. In order to have self-respect, you have to stand up for yourself and your beliefs whether other people like them (or you) or not.

It's okay if some people don't like you. What matters is that the people you love and respect understand you and love you, even if they disagree with your beliefs or the causes you support. Then you can be yourself and not worry about what you say and do or what others are saying or thinking of you. You will have screened out those whom you shouldn't have in your inner circle just by allowing yourself to be authentic.

If you come from integrity, when you make a mistake you take immediate steps to correct it. You'll respect yourself for doing so and you can come out of hiding. Integrity is freedom.

To paraphrase Gandhi, happiness is when what you say, think and do are the same.

# Integrity
*my experience*

I could have told a lie today that would have kept my daughter from some serious heartache, but the truth serum practically jumped out of my toolbox and hit me in the conscience.

I made it her responsibility to fill out and send in the application for an audition at the prestigious School For The Arts, in Florida. She'd been a student there throughout middle school, and according to Nicole's teachers she was a shoo-in for placement at Dreyfus, the arts high school, the following year. Problem is, she got herself into a mess by procrastinating, and it cost her the spot because she missed the application deadline. I could have lied to the admissions department and said I'd sent the application in on time and it must have gotten lost in the mail, etc., etc. Believe me, I considered it. I really wanted her to attend the high school connected to the middle school where she enjoyed her art training over the past few years. She had friends there. She did well there. She thrived there.

But she's done this before. She procrastinates constantly, and so far nothing has taught her a lesson. If I'd jumped in and tried to save her I'd be reinforcing her procrastinating, condoning lying, and interfering with her karma while destroying my own. It had taken me nearly fifty-eight years to "get it," but I finally did. There's nothing worth compromising one's integrity. Doing so affects every cell in your body and clouds your mind with self-doubt, self-loathing and misery, whether you know it or not.

When faced with the possibility of lying, I knew that a lie would screw up my serenity. I knew it with unshakable certainty.

I knew it as a Truth, a Law of the Universe, and it was out of the question. Yet, for a moment I considered it. The very second I made the decision NOT to lie, the heaviness I'd been feeling disappeared and my lightness returned.

What did I learn from this and what is it that I want to share with you?

BE your own truth. Cover for nobody. Even our children have to live according to their own "mistakes." That's how they learn, and sometimes they (and we) only learn when the lessons are very costly. We are ENTITLED to our own lessons. They are our learning tools on Earth.

Give your children the opportunity to cry over life's unexpected disappointing twists now so they don't have to die over them later.

# A Gift to Yourself

Want to give yourself a gift that keeps on giving? It's easy. Make it your purpose today to notice everything for which you can be grateful. I don't just mean the obvious, like winning the lottery or having the folks from The Publishers' Clearinghouse Sweepstakes show up at your house with a check for ten million dollars. I mean having gratitude for such gifts as your abilities, your car, your friends, your clothing and the food on your table. When you make it your purpose to look for reasons to be appreciative you'll find them everywhere, from your ability to open your eyes in the morning to having a bed to sleep in at night. That timer in your toolbox is there to remind you to express gratitude. To get the most out of this gift, set it to go off every hour. The timer bell will force you to think of aspects of yourself and your life that you may be taking for granted.

Why is gratitude the gift that keeps on giving? Gratitude increases dopamine, a feel-good chemical in your brain. When it's increased you feel happier, more alive, and more connected to the world. That's just part of the story. What you really need to remember is that *the Universe hears no negatives!* For instance, when you say, "I wish I didn't have such a big ass," all the Universe hears is "big ass," so it gives you more of it! If you're frequently thinking or saying you're unhappy, poor, stupid, lazy, fat, etc., the Universe gives you more unhappiness, poverty, stupidity, laziness or (OMG!!) fat!!!

If you come from gratitude for what you have, however, the Universe will give you more for which to be grateful. Whatever you want to bring into your life is what you should focus on, but you have to be grateful for your ability to get it. For example, you wouldn't say, "I wish I didn't have scrawny legs," because the Universe hears only "scrawny legs." Instead say, "Thank you God, for giving me great legs with which to walk and dance." You have to make it a HABIT to stay focused on what's good in your life so the WAY you think will begin to change. That's why it's important to set your timer to go off so often, at least until the habit is formed. Forming habits requires consistency. You'll feel a little lift in your spirit from the first moment you acknowledge your gratitude. The more you focus on your blessings, the more blessings will come into your life.

Feeling gratitude without expressing it is like wrapping a gift without giving it. Express it to God, the Source, the Universe, the All, or whatever you want to call the Life Force. You can even express it to someone else. The important part is that you put your gratitude out there in the Universe.

When you live in gratitude you're always happy. When you live in a state of wanting you're always unhappy, and even if you get what you want, if you aren't grateful for what you've got you most likely won't be grateful for what you get. Gratitude is a CONSCIOUS CHOICE. Make that choice and the gift is yours.

For example, think of your honey as your knight in shining armor even though he's really just the guy in the magenta Bermuda shorts, and be grateful for him.

# A Gift to Yourself

*my experience*

Two days ago my daughter called me from school in New York. She was crying so much she could barely speak. Her boyfriend had broken up with her and it was the first time she'd been rejected in a romantic situation. She wanted to come home to Florida immediately. It was a Thursday and she didn't have Friday classes. I told Nikki I was barely able to understand her through her crying, that I was at lunch with a friend, and that I'd call her back as soon as I finished. When I spoke with her after lunch she still hadn't calmed down. She said she had enough airline points to get home to Florida, but not enough to get back to school on Monday. I agreed to split the ticket price with her and said I'd call her when I got home and found an inexpensive flight for her Monday return to New York.

Once on the Internet travel sites, I tried calling her to get approval for flight times and airports, but she didn't answer the phone. Given Nicole's history of hospitalizations following her dad's suicide, I was concerned, as she hadn't been this unhinged in years. After about five calls to her, all of which were unanswered, I went from worried to frustrated to angry. When Nikki finally picked up the phone I told her how much I resented her ignoring my calls after she'd made it sound so urgent that I call her the moment I got home. That's when she told me that her roommate, Elizabeth, had walked into their apartment about half an hour after Nikki had spoken to me, and that Elizabeth's friend had been killed in a car accident that morning.

Nikki didn't answer the phone because she was giving her full attention to Elizabeth and was refocused on Elizabeth's sorrow. She no longer wanted to come home for the weekend, as she didn't want to leave her roommate alone. When I spoke with Nikki the following day, her attitude about her own pain was entirely different than it had been just hours before.

Apparently, just as the girls finished talking, Nikki's timer went off, reminding her to be grateful for her own friends. She felt so much better after giving herself the gift of gratitude, and she spoke to me about realizing the relative insignificance of her sorrow when compared to the finality of Elizabeth's loss. (I slipped that timer into her toolbox before she went to New York. I'm grateful it wasn't ticking when she went through the security line.)

The next afternoon Nikki phoned me. Our conversation follows:

"Hi Nikki."

"Mom, guess where I am?"

"You found Ben and Jerry and you're holding them hostage?"

"No, Mom. I'm on a date with this gorgeous model I met a few months ago. He's in the bathroom now, but I wanted you to know I'm doing fine and I'll call you when I get home."

"So, are you over Superman?" I asked.

"Oh, definitely. I have to go; he's coming back to the table."

"Just tell me how Elizabeth is," I said.

"Much better," she replied. "We're so grateful to have one another, Mom. We're helping each other get through the weekend."

Even in the worst of times, if you count all your blessings as assets you'll show a profit. God gave you a gift of eighty-six thousand, four hundred seconds today. Have you used even one of them to say "Thank you"?

# PART ONE

Your mission, should you decide to accept it...

1. Acknowledge your issues and their impact on your perceptions
2. Pay attention to patterns of behavior
3. Stay away from red flags that signal caution
4. Practice staying in the NOW
5. Rid yourself of the concept of failure
6. Wait twenty-four hours before expressing anger
7. Choose integrity
8. Frequently express gratitude

# Part Two:
## On Responsibility
Great tools to help you with these lessons:

1. **MITTENS:** so you can't point the finger of blame at anyone

2. **EIGHTEEN INCH ROPE:** enough to tie you in knots but not to jump to conclusions

3. **DUCT TAPE:** to cover your mouth when someone is speaking

4. **ERASER:** to eliminate the words *You made me feel...*

5. **PLIERS:** to open your mind to new information

6. **RELATIVES:** to remind you that *normal* is a relative term

7. **MAGNET:** to bring your awareness to times U are about to attach to anger

8. **STOP SIGN:** to remind you to stop and think before saying yes

# The Goldfish Made Me Do It

Ever listen to kids talk? They blame everything on other people: Joey made me eat the cookies, Sasha said I should light the match, Janette told me to take the teacher's notebook.

It's brutal to listen to them blame everyone else for their unacceptable behavior. What's worse, however, is what I don't hear. I don't hear parents telling their kids that nobody can MAKE them behave badly. I don't hear parents explaining to their kids that they have CHOICES, and that they alone are responsible for the choices they make. Those mittens in your toolbox will make it difficult, if not impossible, to point the finger of blame, so tell your kids about them and help them start their own toolboxes.

Teach your children that nobody else can MAKE them do or say anything. But can you really blame kids for making excuses? After all, they so frequently hear adults making statements like, "She made me cry" or, "He made me angry." Except in the case of abuse from which escape is not physically possible, nobody can make you do anything or feel any way unless you're a willing participant. Many who are battered physically are capable of removing themselves from the abuser, but CHOOSE to stay out of fear. Sometimes that fear is so overwhelming it feels as if there's no choice but to stay. Remember, feelings aren't facts.

It's not just a matter of semantics. If you believe people can make you feel or act a certain way, you're always at the mercy of others.  If you feel awful about  something you've done, take responsibility for it.  When you take ownership of your actions you can control them, change them, make them better.

Before your kids place blame on other people for their mistakes, teach them to always count to ten...ten of their own.

# The Goldfish Made Me Do It

*my experience*

Back in the seventies I took a weekend course called EST (Erhard Seminar Training). I was in my twenties and had never thought about the concept of taking responsibility for my own actions. I don't think people even used the term "taking responsibility" in those days. The seminar was all about changing people's thoughts so they'd perceive reality differently and could thereby change their lives. I longed to change mine.

At one point, and I'll never forget this because I was stumped over the concept for years, the trainer asked, "If a pedestrian is crossing the street and a bus hits her, is it the responsibility of the pedestrian or the bus?" To me, the answer was clearly *the bus*, but the EST trainer said it was the responsibility of the pedestrian. I was so confused by the reasoning behind the answer, and so utterly perplexed about most of what the other two hundred ninety-nine people at the seminar seemed to grasp, that I cried my eyes out.

Everybody in the group went around saying, "Did you get it?" The question was met with bright eyes and huge smiles; "I got it!" was always the answer, or at least that's how I perceived it. I didn't know what "it" was, but apparently *getting IT* was what the seminar was all about. People of all ages returned from these seminars saying their lives had been transformed for the better. I felt so much worse. "Left out again," I thought, not realizing at the time that "left out" was one of my issues.

Follow me here. The reasoning behind the answer is that there's no such thing as fault, there's just "what is." Initially, when the trainer asked, "...whose responsibility is it...?" I heard the word *fault* and missed his purposeful use of the word *responsibility. Fault* and *responsibility* are words created by us to qualify behavior. WE CREATED the concept of FAULT. *Fault* is a judgment that keeps us from seeing life as it is: just actions and behaviors with nothing added (no judgments). Although the EST trainer said it was the *responsibility* of the pedestrian, I was still hearing *fault*. My stubborn brain wasn't letting me exchange *fault* for *responsibility.* This, by the way, is my explanation, which is put in reasonable terms, I hope. We were told that nothing in the seminar was reasonable because nothing in life is reasonable. It just IS what it is. Again, we give things meaning, without which all words and events would be neutral.

If we substitute the word *fault,* which doesn't help us in any way (except if you're in the legal system), and replace it with the word *responsibility,* our lives will change because *fault* is placing blame, which is a hard pill to swallow, while *responsibility* is a neutral word, so it's easier to accept. It doesn't have the same negative connotation as *fault.*

Going back to the question about the bus, I couldn't accept, or even understand, how there could be no fault, no judgment, no condemnation of anyone or anything for such an incident. Who should be blamed? I didn't want to give up being able to blame, so I wasn't "getting it."

If there were no judgments, no blame and no concept of fault, we could then say that we are responsible for everything that happens in our lives. We're not *blamed* for anything; it's just that we were there, so we are *responsible.* You may find this a stretch, but forget about *fault* and just focus on the action. A bus is going down the street and somehow you put yourself in front of it. Therefore, you are *responsible* for being in front of the bus at the very moment the bus was going down the street.

The point is, blaming ourselves or others does nothing to help us make our lives better, but TAKING RESPONSIBILITY for everything we do allows us to examine all our experiences from a non-judgmental viewpoint. As such, we can recognize our part in why events occur. It's only then that we can see our patterns of behavior and trace how our actions lead to certain results. If we stop thinking it's our *fault,* and start seeing everything as *just what it is,* we can more easily see our behaviors clearly and stop blaming either others or ourselves.

For example, all my romantic relationships failed in my early years. I felt powerless to change my patterns because I always believed the problems in the relationships were the other person's fault. That's what prompted me to add mittens to my toolbox and that's why I'm giving them to you. I don't know how I lived without them. Actually, I do know: I was cold.

I consistently chose men who outwardly seemed self-confident, successful and interestingly complex. Emotionally, however, they were insecure, needy and controlling. When I looked at the relationships as a series of behaviors, each person being responsible for his or her own, I could see that I was responsible for choosing the same kind of person over and over again, so I was allowing certain elements within the relationships to remain the same in all of them. Because I wasn't getting what I expected, which were the men I PERCEIVED them to be, I was invariably disappointed and felt cheated. This was MY issue because I usually felt disappointed and cheated as a child, so I unconsciously chose men with whom I'd continue to feel disappointed and cheated because they were the only ones in my comfort zone. When I could see my part in these failed relationships I was able to change the type of man I chose, and therefore, change the nature of my relationships.

Instead of blaming others for being overly sensitive or for creating the drama that made my life crazy, I saw that it was I who CHOSE the people in my life and I who was responsible for CHOOSING different kinds of guys in the future if I wanted my life to change. I saw my patterns because I was LOOKING INSIDE myself.

We can't change anyone else, and blaming someone in order to make ourselves right does nothing to help either party. In fact, blaming always makes relationships worse. The single most powerful change I've ever made was taking responsibility for everything that happens in my life.  As a result, my whole life has changed.

You have the power to change your life right now.  We already have a Bill of Rights, now all we need is a Bill of Responsibilities.

# Jumping To Conclusions

Is your favorite sport jumping to conclusions?

We've all experienced making up our own little stories about what's behind someone's behavior; usually it's behavior that ticks us off.

For example, last week while my friend Ruth was doing errands she saw her boyfriend's car, so she beeped and waved for him to stop and pull over. But he didn't pull over. They had been having a little tiff, and Ruth was sure she was being "dissed" because of it. She was livid. For two days steam came out of her ears as she obsessed over being ignored.

Then, on the third day her boyfriend called just like nothing had happened. Turns out, her boyfriend's cousin, whom Ruth had never met, was driving her honey's car. Ruth felt relieved to find out her beaux hadn't ignored her, but she also felt a little ridiculous for jumping to a conclusion that infuriated her and could have ruined her relationship. And I was just about to give her that eighteen-inch rope! It could have reminded her that when she's all tied up in knots she shouldn't jump to conclusions.

From time to time, we all jump to conclusions. Maybe you don't hear from a friend for a while and you jump to the conclusion that he's mad at you, only to find out later he's had the flu and was sleeping for two days. Or when your son comes home for dinner late you might decide that means he doesn't respect you, so you greet him angrily and reprimand him immediately. Later you realize your cell phone's been off, and when you check your messages you confirm that he called earlier to say he had to wait for his friend's mom to give him a ride home.

Whenever you're stressed and your stomach feels like its tied up in knots, remember that the rope is only eighteen inches; not long enough to jump to conclusions. Get the facts instead of making up your own story, and never attribute to malice that which can be adequately explained by circumstance.

# Jumping To Conclusions

*my experience*

Look at the girl in this picture. Doesn't she look great? Thin, happy, pretty, right? Looks like she has it all together.

WRONG!!

That's me when I was thirty-one years old. I was a tortured soul back then.

I was out of my most dangerous anorexic stage, but still completely obsessed with my weight. I was using amphetamines and cocaine to kill whatever appetite I had, and was taking pills to calm me down at night so I could sleep.

I was constantly comparing myself to others. If I was in a restaurant, for example, and there was a beautiful girl at the next table, I was fixated on her. If she looked "cool," I scanned what she was wearing so I could copy her style. Whenever I was in the vicinity of a girl whom I perceived to be beautiful, I was so intimidated I could barely function. My mind chattered away 24/7.

Nevertheless, people thought I was having the time of my life. Just look at me. Why wouldn't I be?

When you look at the women and men modeling in magazines, or at movie stars or at your friends' seemingly perfect relationships, don't jump to conclusions, and don't believe your own made up stories. Trust me.

# Can You Top This?

Are you in the habit of playing "Can you top this?" When someone tells you about the very worst day she's ever had in her entire life, do you say something like, "Wait until you hear about MY day"?

Any response that doesn't show empathy for the person confiding in you is likely to be just another crummy experience in an already lousy day. Even though it may be human nature to do so, don't judge, act shocked or show body language negativity; no grimaces or raised eyebrows when someone spills her guts to you. She might just need a hug and the words, "I'm sorry you had such a bad day."

If you relate to interrupting others to get your two cents in (and you probably do it without even knowing you do), get out the duct tape and place it securely over your mouth so you don't interrupt. That will also make it a whole lot easier to resist the urge to say, "I understand," because the other person may say or feel that you couldn't possibly understand. In fact, don't use the word "I" at all, because that person's problem isn't about you! Contrary to what appears to be popular opinion, when someone takes a breath, it doesn't mean the person is either finished talking or has a speech impediment!

BTW, those who always interrupt with their stories of how they did more, saw more or ate more usually have big egos and low self-esteem, and big egos have small ears.

When there's a lengthy pause, a helpful response to the gut-spiller is to briefly paraphrase what the person has said and make a statement about the emotion you OBSERVE. For example, "So you're *concerned* that your parents may become dependent on you for their finances." Or, "Sounds like the reassignments at work are causing you *worry*." Just sum things up in a sentence or two, and then let the other person continue to vent.

The most important action you can take is putting your own ego on hold and listening with your whole heart. The gift of really listening and empathizing is one nobody can top!

# Can You Top This?

*my experience*

Over the course of my lifetime I've met so many people who could top anything I ever did or said. It's not difficult to top my experiences, especially when it comes to traveling. I've wanted to travel to far away, exotic places, but if New Jersey doesn't qualify, I'm not going to play the "Can You Top This?" game. When I talk about going to New York and someone responds by telling me about the breathtaking scenery in Alaska or the like, I feel like my own New York trip wasn't even worthy of acknowledgment to the listener. That's MY issue, and it circles back to the period in my life when I felt cheated because I neither had what the other kids had, nor did what they did. (See how often early feelings keep coming up in different circumstances?)

I've listened to hundreds, if not thousands of tales of adventures and intrigue over the years, and I've noticed that people are always trying to top each other when it comes to... well..., everything!

Some people just don't consider the listener's feelings when they speak. If someone said, "I've never owned a gown," would a thoughtful person reply, "I have so many gowns I can't get them all in my closets," and then go on to describe them for the next twenty minutes? If Sally were to say, "My husband (boyfriend, girlfriend, wife) has never given me a piece of jewelry," is it kind for another person to go on and on about the thirty-five amazing necklaces her somewhat significant other gave her?

Even if someone talks about feeling sick, there's always a person who wants you to know he nearly died. If you're upset because you bumped your head when you had a fender bender, someone pops up to tell you he or she was in a coma for twenty-seven days after being trampled by a herd of elephants.

Every once in a while I catch myself doing the same kind of thing, but it doesn't feel to me as though I'm trying to "top" someone else. Nevertheless, while it doesn't FEEL that way to me, the person with whom I'm talking probably wants to bitch slap me! From now on, I think I'll use the duct tape just in case.

While it's human nature to come from the ego sometimes, it's not pretty. We all want to share our experiences, but one of the challenges of communicating is to suspend our egos and just listen. It behooves us to at least comment on the other person's experience before sharing our own.

BTW, if you happen to be one of the people who've described to me the fantastic stories of your many globe-trotting adventures, you should know that I'm not the egotistical person who would try to top you by booking an extended trip around the world... not that there's a lack of requests for me to do so.

# Four Damaging Words

Four of the most damaging words used in relationships are, "You made me feel..." In the first place, as you know, NOBODY can MAKE you feel any way. People do what they do and you feel what you feel when they do it. Look at these phrases and see which one feels like an attack:

You made me feel insignificant when you put my name last on the list.

or

I feel insignificant when I'm last on the list.

The first sentence is a blaming statement which feels like an attack and prompts the listener to either defend himself or attack back. In the second sentence the speaker is stating a fact about himself and taking responsibility for his own feelings. There's no reason for the listener to strike back or defend since there was no attack. Instead, the other person can actually HEAR what's being said.

If you don't want to be heard, attack people by telling them how bad they made you feel. They'll stop listening the minute you say, "You made me feel..." because they'll be thinking of how to counterattack. It's human nature to defend oneself. If you wouldn't physically attack someone, why would you do it emotionally? When you use those four words you make yourself someone's puppet. What you're really saying is that someone else controls you. Don't give anyone the power to pull your strings. Get out your eraser again and eliminate those four boring, monosyllabic, trouble-causing words!

Only when you take ownership of your feelings do you have the POWER TO CHANGE them. There's always something YOU can do.

To put it another way, if your only means of transportation is your bike, but it isn't safe and can't be fixed, you can always get a louder horn.

# Four Damaging Words
*my experience*

The single most damaging behavior to me and my relationships has probably been blaming other people for how I felt. That's why I have such high praise for the usually underrated eraser! Just one erasure and the words, *You made me feel...* Gone! Like a little mosquito that ran into the flame of a citronella candle, neither the words nor the mosquito will ever bite me in the you-know-where again.

Until I really "got" that I alone was responsible for everything I experienced, I didn't have good relationships. I was never able to get past blaming others so I was unable to see that I was responsible for my feelings. As a result, I wasn't learning anything that could benefit me in future relationships. I kept LOOKING FOR the same kinds of people; those who didn't ruffle my feathers, so to speak.

It never occurred to me that if I didn't figure out a way to keep my feathers from ruffling I'd never be able to fly. I was stuck being a victim.

After I had internalized the concept of personal responsibility, whenever I felt hurt, for example, I explained to my friends that what I was feeling was not a reflection of someone else's behavior, but rather, a reflection of my own past. Despite having difficulty giving up blame earlier in my life, I was surprised when, years later, my friends resisted the concept. Whenever I told a story in which I wasn't angry at someone else for a situation I'd created, they'd make statements like, "But she did...TO YOU" or, "You wouldn't have done...if he hadn't done...TO YOU." They simply didn't want to let others off the hook. After all, if someone else isn't responsible for a problem, who is?

Now, if somebody gets upset with me I don't automatically apologize as I once did. Taking responsibility for myself has enabled me to stop taking responsibility for how others feel. What a huge relief! This mindset also freed me from guilt. Ta-dah!

It's great to be able to tell people how I feel about what they say or do without making my feelings their fault. They can listen without being defensive since I'm sharing feelings about myself (why I'm sensitive about certain things based on my past), rather than accusing others of being insensitive, rude, thoughtless, etc., all of which creates distance, not closeness.

People who take ownership of their feelings and behaviors, placing no blame on others, have remained in my life. They're willing to share their feelings and histories in order to explain their sensitivities, and they know I won't feel blamed for how they feel, even if it's in the context of something I did or said. Our relationships become closer when we take responsibility for everything we say and do. Saying, "I feel this way because you..." tears relationships apart. Instead, say, "When...happens, I feel..."

Children are taught to either blame others or take ownership of their feelings. They mimic their parents. There are, however, a few exceptions. For instance, I've noticed that kids never mimic their parents using a vacuum cleaner or unloading a dishwasher. They do, however, repeat everything their parents should never have said.

# Changing Course

Do you know that once you've made your mind up about something it's next to impossible to change your opinion? In fact, we tend to ignore evidence that supports opposing opinions and consistently NOTICE whatever we think supports the ones we've previously formed. So get out your pliers, because you'll need an open mind if you're going to grow. Some minds are more tightly closed than others, so if necessary, keep prying.

Consider an experiment that has been replicated many times in different ways, but always gets the same results. When a group of Democrats and a group of Republicans watched a film about political policy outcomes, the Democrats evaluated the content of the film as biased in favor of the Democrats, while the Republicans evaluated the same film as biased in favor of the Republicans!

Think of all the times your own prejudices interfered with conclusions you drew and how you reacted as a result of your already biased, and perhaps, rigid opinions. For example, if you believe that dark-skinned people are lousy drivers, whenever a dark-skinned person cuts you off, you'll take that as evidence that your belief is justified. If you don't hold any firm belief about light-skinned drivers, when one cuts you off you'll either ignore it, get annoyed, or become furious and do something stupid to get even. But since there's no *category* in your brain labeled *Light-Skinned Drivers Stink,* you won't store the experience as *proof* that you're right. Can you imagine the amount of evidence you've stored through the years supporting opinions you decided were *right* long ago? Have you changed your opinions when presented with evidence to refute what those opinions were based on?

Consider the possibility that you may not have even seen or heard the evidence to the contrary. Perhaps you haven't been exposed to it, or when you were, you didn't notice it and just passed it by. Unless we're aware of our tendency to ignore what we don't accept or believe, we automatically screen it out. What we consider *common sense* is just a compilation of feelings and ideas our families, communities, schools, etc. teach us to believe, plus prejudices we absorb from our like-minded friends. As such, our notion of common sense may have distinctly limiting effects on our perceptions of reality.

Sometimes people stick to their opinions and can't seem to get unstuck, even in the face of new facts or absolute proof to the contrary. If you're not willing to change your mind, you're not willing to grow. If you think of intelligence as fixed, you're less likely to be open to learning new information than if you think of it as ever-expanding, which it is. A mind is like a parachute; it only serves you if it's open.

# Changing Course
*my experience*

Once we've formed opinions about someone or something, opposing evidence doesn't stand a chance. There were a few people in my life about whom much evidence opposing my opinions continued to mount for months, and sometimes even years, before I was willing to admit to myself that I was wrong about them. I clung to my opinions for two reasons: first, I wanted to believe the opinions I formed initially were justified because I was getting something I valued from the relationship, like a good friend or a boyfriend, and second, every once in a while these people would do or say something that validated my good feelings about them. Then they'd win me over and I'd lose the argument with myself about leaving them. My belief in these folks continued despite their thoughtless behavior or lies because I was on what psychologists call a variable-intermittent reinforcement schedule, in which every so often some goodie came my way, but I never knew when it was coming, so I was hooked. These relationships were to me as slot machines are to gamblers.

As far as previous boyfriends are concerned, it was always my friends who first saw what I defended over and over again. It was one thing not to admit to myself I was wrong about someone, but after I'd defended a person's behavior to other people who "told me so" for years, it was painful to have to admit how wrong I'd been. In retrospect, the evidence that these people were bad news was obvious. Was I blind? Why was I willing to accept a little crumb now and then? Why didn't my opinion of these people change automatically as a result of their behavior towards me?

In order to change my opinions I had to re-evaluate myself to UNDERSTAND WHY I was willing to put up with so little for so long. I had to go into my soul and admit to myself that I didn't believe I was worth more; more respect, more consideration, more loyalty. The painful part was figuring out why I had such low self-esteem.

While finding myself was a process that included learning the lessons in this book, just admitting to myself how little I believed I was worth helped me to change course. Then, in order to head in the right direction, I made a list of the qualities I valued in a partner and those I valued in a friend. I made a conscious CHOICE to change course each time I recognized my old, self-destructive patterns. While my initial attraction to healthy guys wasn't nearly as strong as it was to the men I'd previously chosen, I continued trying and prying. Finally, I've grown into genuine mutual love with a man who treats me like a rare gem. Chemistry alone is not a good indicator that someone is Mr. Right, or even Mr. Close Enough. For me, the greater the respect I felt, the greater the chemistry. Once my respect was EARNED OVER TIME, THEN his great sense of humor, kindness and intelligence delighted me a thousand fold, AND the attraction was magnetic. New insights about myself and a list of well thought-out characteristics that are important to me in a friend and a significant other enabled me to change course. But human beings have to want to change direction. Misery can be a good motivator for change. When you're really motivated, new positive input can help you change course if it's powerful enough. You just have to open your mind, make a decision to accept new information and, with an "I can and I will" attitude, go where it leads you. The most important part is that you TAKE THE ACTION REQUIRED to change course.

If you realize you're going in the wrong direction, don't procrastinate or stick to your guns just to be *right* in the eyes of others. To illustrate this point, check out the actual radio conversation released by Captain Hail, the Chief of U.S. Naval Operations, on October 15, 1995. It follows below.

Hail: Please divert your course fifteen degrees to the North to avoid a collision.

Reply: Recommend you change YOUR course fifteen degrees to the South to avoid a collision.

Hail: This is the Captain of a U.S. Navy ship. I say again, divert YOUR course.

Reply: No! I say again divert YOUR course.

Hail: THIS IS THE AIRCRAFT CARRIER ENTERPRISE. WE ARE A LARGE WARSHIP OF THE U.S. NAVY. DIVERT YOUR COURSE NOW.

Reply: This is a lighthouse...Your call.

# Normal Misery

Have you ever felt so sad, hopeless or depressed that you wondered if what you felt was "normal"?

What's normal depends on where you're coming from, and I don't mean Ohio or Philadelphia. To my way of thinking, giving a name to a specific cluster of behaviors may be helpful to the diagnostician, but not to the client. Most labels delineate too rigid a framework to include the individual differences that reflect each person's unique experiences. *Normal* only means something is the norm; what most people do or feel. It doesn't address or include assessing the client's individual background and history IN RELATION TO those behaviors and thoughts.

For example, if you feel terrified by confrontations of any kind no matter how small, that may be abnormal in general, but if every time your parents argued their fights became violent or hurtful confrontations, or if outbursts towards you frequently resulted in disturbing consequences that negatively impacted your life, it would be normal for you to fear confrontation. You have to look at the picture of your relatives in your toolbox when you're questioning your sanity. It will remind you that *normal* is a relative term. Painful memories often reside very close to the surface and can be activated by events or scenes that resemble them no matter how long ago you experienced the original pain.

Is it normal to become anxious every time you go to a playground? Of course not. However, if as a child you had to wear ugly orthopedic shoes for a couple of years to correct a deformity, and if the other kids on the playground made fun of you or your shoes, you'd associate the playground with the feelings you had when people made fun of you there. GIVEN YOUR HISTORY, anxiety about going to playgrounds would be normal.

If you become sad or depressed and wonder if it's normal to feel the way you do, consider all the events that may have contributed to your misery and ask yourself if under the same circumstances other people would probably feel the same way. You may be surprised how often the answer is in the affirmative. The misery you feel may not be normal for people who've never had your experiences, but you might be surprised how easily you can see why it's normal FOR YOU, UNDER THE CIRCUMSTANCES.

However, if your misery is so severe or long-lasting (about three months or more) that it significantly impairs the way you function at work or at home, it's probably time to talk to a professional who may be able to teach you some techniques to break the cycle of depression. The longer the misery goes on, the more the neurons in your brain go down the *misery path*. If the neurons travel down the same pathway often enough they become deeply etched in your nervous system, and the greater the chances of you forming the habits of perpetually depressed people. These habits include isolating yourself, becoming sedentary, no longer caring about your health and your appearance and changes in your patterns of eating and sleeping (either more or less than usual). Frequent early morning awakenings can also be a red flag. If you feel sad or hopeless for a couple of months it may be time to get some help, especially if you experience one or more of the symptoms mentioned.

Generally speaking though, it's often normal to be abnormal.

# Normal Misery
*my experience*

When my son was about two, I had lunch with a psychiatrist friend of mine. She said I looked exhausted and asked me what was wrong.

"I feel like my life is over," I told her. "My son does nothing but cry. I can't do anything to please him. I'm up with him most of the night so I'm exhausted every morning. I chase him around all day constantly cleaning up his poop and I have to fight to get him to nap. I have no energy left for anything mundane, no less anything that's fun. I have no time for myself, not even to take a shower!"

I began to cry as I was about to make one of the most difficult confessions of my life. "I feel like I hate him," I said.

My psychiatrist friend didn't even look up from her sushi. I'd just said something terrible and she didn't even blink!

"Did you hear what I said?" I asked.

"Sure," she answered. "Of course you hate him. What's there to like?"

And with that one comment, she made it all okay.

"Of course," I thought. "How else COULD I feel?"

It was a huge relief to give myself permission to hate the little terror responsible for my sleep-deprived, lackluster life. That's when I came to the realization that the purpose of throwing children's parties is to remind yourself that there are children more awful than your own.

As Jesse got older (much older), my feelings changed, but there were still times when I just didn't like my kids. In fact, sometimes I couldn't stand them. I'm sure there were many times they couldn't stand me either.

From time to time it's normal to dislike your kids, spouse, partner, friends, parents, or anyone else close to you. When it happens don't freak out. Examine the situation. Does it make sense to you that you'd feel loving in those circumstances? If the answer is *no*, you're probably having a normal response to your perceived situation.

What's important is that your feelings are the result of circumstances and not the relationship itself. However, if the feelings go on long enough, you may have to re-evaluate your part in the relationship.

Nothing in life ever stays the same. Difficult situations come and go. When clients leave my office feeling miserable, I say, "Don't get used to it; it won't last."

When they leave my office feeling elated, I say exactly the same thing.

To put it another way, you have to accept the fact that some days you're the pigeon and some days you're the statue.

# On Being Angry

Ever ask someone if he or she thinks your anger about something is justified? Think about that. If you're mad, you're mad. You don't need anyone else to give you permission to be angry or to validate your feelings. Feel what you feel! Let yourself feel all your feelings. What's important is that you don't ACT impulsively on your feelings!

Some people remind me of anger magnets. They're just waiting to find something to cling to; something to which they can attach their anger. These folks will always be mad about something; what they see on T.V., what they hear somewhere, what they read, or what someone else does. These anger magnets are already mad and they seek out any excuse to act out their rage. The magnet in your toolbox is there to remind you to pull away from situations in which you seem magnetically drawn to anger. A good example is how some people react to drivers who are too slow, in the wrong lane or texting while driving. The angry person's reactions are spontaneous and impulsive. The minute you start to attach yourself to anger, get out that U shaped magnet to remind U that nothing good can come from what U are about to do.

Most of us carry some anger associated with past experiences. When you get angry because you feel slighted or disrespected, for example, ask yourself if you OFTEN feel slighted or disrespected. If so, see if you can figure out when those feelings originated by asking yourself, "At what other time in my life did I feel...?"

(Fill in the name of your feeling, such as stupid, unappreciated, intimidated, etc.) Frequently they originate in childhood.

Years ago a woman client who'd felt abandoned and angry as a child found herself feeling exactly the same way forty years later. During our first session I asked her why she thought she was reliving those feelings. She replied, "The psychologist I've gone to for thirty years just died on me."

"She didn't die ON YOU," I said, "she just died."

So often we make everything all about ourselves. We need to get out of our own way to *separate what happens from our feelings about what happens.* Most of the time when we get angry, nobody is doing anything TO US; they're just doing what they're doing, and if we get angry it's because of what's inside of us.

Whatever you do, don't act on anger until you've taken a time-out.

Remember, danger is only one short letter away from anger.

# On Being Angry
*my experience*

This photo was taken at the beautiful Vizcaya Gardens in Florida, just before my second wedding.

It's a painful picture for me to look at because I was high as a kite, and my dear father was probably trying to make sense of whatever nonsense I was saying. Just look at my left fist clenched in anger, and at my wedding! I have no recollection of what this exchange was about, but I behaved horribly that weekend, locking myself in my room, taking all sorts of pills to hype me

I Can Relate To That!

up then slow me down, and consciously trying to be unconscious during a wedding I knew should never have taken place.

This photo shows my anger, but I'm sure I blamed it on everyone and everything outside myself. I had "reasons" for everything I did, including drugging. I never took responsibility for anything in those days. I escaped into drugs so I didn't have to experience the disappointment and hurt I'd held inside for so long. I was definitely an anger magnet. I was angry with myself, but didn't know it until I had been sober for a while.

I've often heard people in Twelve-Step Programs say they didn't know they had choices. We have choices about everything, but we give up something for each choice we make. At first, it didn't FEEL as though I had the choice to be sober. But as the Twelve-Step Programs teach, feelings aren't facts.

When I CHOSE to be sober and clear my mind, I gave up my excuses and took responsibility for my misery and anger. Only then was my unhappiness under my own control. Today I consciously make the choice to be happy every single day, and for me that includes not acting on anger...except when I do. (Get real!!)

For example, I was angry when my computer beat me at chess, but I didn't let it bother me in the least; it was no match for me at kickboxing.

# Learning To Say No

Do you have trouble saying "No" to people? If so, go to your toolbox and fish out that STOP sign, because you really need it. If you always say "Yes" because you don't want to disappoint people and you find yourself feeling resentful, try this:

When asked to do anything at all, say, "Let me think about that and get back to you."

You'll then have time to consider how you actually FEEL about doing what was asked of you, and you can DECIDE if you have the time and energy to take on the task. Of course there are times when an immediate response is appropriate, but in most cases you do have the option to reflect on how you feel and make a thoughtful decision. You'll be healthier and happier for doing so. The STOP sign is in your toolbox to remind you to stop and think before you answer questions requiring a *yes* or *no* response.

Remember, everything takes energy, so ask yourself, "Will this drain me of the energy I could be using on something more important in my life?"

The respect of others is earned by being honest, and saying *no* is acceptable. You might add, "I'm not comfortable with that" or, "The timing just isn't good for me."

The ability to say *no* is critical to your self-respect, self-esteem and well-being.

And think about it; don't you respect people more if they can say *no*?

So, if you're in the habit of saying *yes* right away, change that habit to, "Hmm... let me think about that and get back to you."

# Learning To Say No
*my experience*

I'll never forget the first time I actually heard myself say *no* to someone who asked me to do something I really didn't want to do. Before I learned to say *no*, I'd skirt around the issue, lie about why I couldn't do it, ignore the person who made the request or refuse to answer the phone. There were many times I didn't know how to say *no,* so I said, "I'll try," and simply didn't show up or do what was asked of me. It never occurred to me that I really COULD say *no.* I guess I didn't think saying *no* was a valid choice. I certainly didn't think it was "nice" to say it.

I was in a Twelve-Step Program, going for therapy twice a week and working on staying healthy when an old flame, associated with my earlier unhealthy habits, phoned and wanted to get together. I knew I might be putting myself in a compromising situation by agreeing to see him. I had worked too hard on changing my life to risk going backwards.

I heard myself say, "Let me think about that and get back to you." It doesn't seem like a big deal now, but at the time it was as if the words came out in slow motion. I could hardly believe I didn't lie or take the cowardly way out and simply agree to meet him. I bought myself time to think it through and to imagine potential scenarios and possible consequences of saying *yes.* I wasn't just procrastinating. I knew this was different. It felt different. I actually INTENDED to think about it. What a concept!

The next day I phoned my former heartthrob and told him my life had changed and getting together was not something I wanted to do. When he tried to convince me to reconsider, I simply said, "Thanks for the invitation, but getting together just doesn't work for me. I'm short on time so I have to go. Be well." Then I hung up, went outside, and found a big red STOP sign at the end of my block. I took a picture of it and had miniature copies of the sign made for our toolboxes.

I sat at my desk for a long while. Did those words really come out of my mouth? I was amazed when they did. This was another step in turning my life around. For a very long time I answered every request by saying, "Let me think about that and get back to you." It was one of the best habits I've ever developed. Now I can say *no* very easily, a fact to which my children can attest.

I've treated many clients over the past twenty years, and in my experience the most difficult word for people to say is *no*. Tommy, my first husband (of forty minutes), was a stockbroker. Before our wedding he wanted to change the words of our marriage ceremony from "for richer or poorer" to "in bull markets or bear markets." Uncharacteristically, I said *no*.

I should have realized then that there was a farewell feel about him.

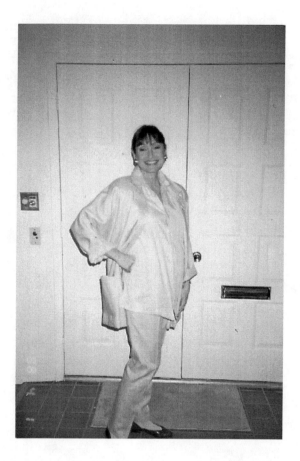

In this picture I'm about eight months pregnant with my son, Jesse. Obviously, I didn't say *no* all the time!

# PART TWO

Your Mission, Should You Decide To Accept It ...

1. Live a no-fault life
2. Make no assumptions
3. Park your ego and focus on the other person
4. Take responsibility for creating everything you say and do
5. Recognize what doesn't work for you and expend energy on what does
6. Think of *normal* in relation to the circumstances
7. Wait twenty-four hours before acting on anger
8. Choose to say *NO* if you don't want to do something

# Part Three:
## On Control
Even more tools for your magical toolbox:

1. **SWORD SHEATH:** to prevent you from hurting anyone

2. **LIFE PRESERVER:** to prevent you from wasting your breath treading water

3. **WHITE FLAG:** to surrender control

4. **CHALK:** to draw your boundaries

5. **ABCs:** to teach others how to treat you

6. **SCALE:** to weigh choices

7. **MIRROR:** to reflect how you want others to treat you

8. **BLANKET:** to cover yourself when you give advice

9. **YIELD SIGN:** to remind you to take time to think of alternatives

# Sword of Silence

Silence can be golden, but it can also feel like violence.

Have you ever been in a relationship with someone who just stops talking when he or she is angry? Maybe you've even done it yourself. Using silence as a weapon or a means of control can be deadly to a relationship. I included the sword sheath in your toolbox to remind you that your sword of silence can cause everyone, including you, pain. Use the sheath to cover that dangerous sword and keep it covered; it's a deadly weapon and can cause your relationship to die a slow and painful death.

You may feel like you're getting even with someone by shutting down, but the person at whom you're angry may not even know what you're mad about. No matter how much people love you they can't read your mind. You may think, "Of course she knows why I'm pouting," but that's because no matter how small the issue behind your anger may be, it's so big TO YOU, you can't believe the other party isn't aware of it. Keep in mind that what's probably happening is YOUR buttons have gotten pushed, not because someone pushed them, but because you've made a CHOICE (albeit unconscious) to allow them to be pushed BY DEFAULT, either by ignoring, denying, or being totally unaware that you have issues that are being activated by something that's going on. That's why it's absolutely essential to know what your issues are!

If you're angry about something, say so. You might say something like, "I felt hurt when you threw that George Foreman grill at my head" or, "I was crushed when you ran over my feet with the SUV." You know...just say what's on your mind. Make it easy. Substitute, "I felt hurt when..." and fill in the blanks.

If you haven't done so in the past, saying how you really feel may be upsetting to others who've never heard you express your true feelings. Even though they probably hated your prolonged passive-aggressive silences, upon hearing how you really feel they may wish you'd have just kept you mouth shut. But this isn't about other people and their comfort; it's about you and your happiness.

Eventually, if you continue to CALMLY speak your mind, your honesty will not only help you find yourself, it will help you weed out those who can't accept you for exactly who you are, and it will help you find those people who'll accept and appreciate a healthier, happier you. But even before you can be honest with others you have to meet the challenge of being honest with yourself.

If you want to know exactly how honest you are with yourself right now, check the zero adjustment on your bathroom scale.

# Sword of Silence
*my experience*

I grew up in a house in which I feared silence. I was about ten through fourteen years of age when my brother was going through his adolescence. Like so many kids my age, I was very sensitive and impressionable. My dad and my brother Bob often clashed, but they didn't talk out their issues; they boiled silently. I stayed neutral with undertones of suppressed rage throughout my childhood and adolescence.

I never knew what mood to expect at the dinner table where we sat down together every weekday night. I remember being afraid to speak and feeling that my pressure-cooker family might explode if I said or did anything that inadvertently turned up the heat. Although these periods of silence didn't occur on a daily basis, I lived in a state of low-grade fear and developed an ongoing anxiety that lasted well into my thirties. This anxiety didn't SEEM to be related to anything in particular since there was nothing going on AT THE TIME that was especially anxiety provoking. Nevertheless, low-grade anxiety or dis-ease was always there making happiness out of my reach.

Until I was in my forties it didn't even occur to me that when I came home from school as a youngster I was often deeply affected by the silent rage energy that filled the house. If my mom was upset about something I could feel it. Yet when asked, she very rarely shared what was bothering her and usually denied the fact that anything was wrong. It was obvious to me, however, from the silence (accompanied by what I call the *silence attitude,* which she adopted with no affect whatsoever when she had to speak, as in, "Dinner is on the table"), that something wasn't right. I absorbed the negative energy like terry cloth.

If we use the silence with which we learned to control others in the past to control those in the present, we have to consider the long-term effects. Not only do we suffer physically, emotionally and spiritually, but no relationship can withstand prolonged or frequent bouts of silence.

If this resonates with you, be aware that after prolonged silences and refusals to admit to anything being wrong, your partners, children and friends will eventually have enough of trying to coax, cajole and baby you into expressing yourself. They'll just turn you off. It's called *habituation.* Your silence becomes a habit for them just as it is for you, and it stops bothering them. They end up ignoring you and most likely, resenting you as well. Then what do you do to "express" your anger? Usually that's the beginning of the end. You might think you're still in a relationship, but you'll soon be asking yourself why you're not feeling the love.

Let's say you're on the other end of the sword and you're married. If your husband or wife suddenly realizes that silence isn't always golden and begins expressing feelings verbally, you might, until you get used to it, be sexually turned off by your newly expressive mate. On the other hand, marriage itself changes things: now you're in bed with a relative!

# Wanting To Be
# Wanted

Ever find out someone doesn't like you and you can't figure out why? Sometimes I see people swimming against the tide, expending so much energy to get someone to like them, but they're just treading water and getting nowhere. Get out your trusty life preserver when you experience this. It's a great addition to your toolbox. Allow the life preserver to come to mind whenever you feel as if you're doing your best and getting nowhere. Better yet, put it on so you can stop wasting your breath.

Ultimately, we have no control over whether someone likes us or not. Obviously, if you're an ax murderer you won't have quite as many friends as the neighborhood Good Samaritan. But even Good Sam can't control whatever reaction someone has to him.

If you're super popular, someone will think you're a phony. If you have lots of money, there'll be those who think you're cheap. Incredibly attractive people are often perceived as stuck up, even from afar.

If somebody doesn't want to like you don't make it your problem. What people think of you has much more to do with whom THEY are than with who you are. THE LESS HAPPY PEOPLE ARE WITH THEMSELVES THE MORE FAULTS THEY FIND WITH OTHERS.

People usually attribute to others the traits they themselves have. For example, some people are so kind they assume everyone is coming from a place of genuine kindness. (Sure she stole my wallet, but she's probably going to give the money to the starving children in India.) People who are angry read hostility into the behavior of others. (Sure she gave the money to the starving children of India, but she only did it to make herself feel better about stealing my wallet.)

If you've acted with integrity and a person simply dislikes you, move on. If he or she spreads rumors or tries to create problems for you, remember it's the other person's hurt, fear, jealousy or anger that's at the root of this behavior, but that person probably doesn't realize it. Everyone is at a different place on this journey, so turn the other cheek in the direction of compassion.

Nobody can be a skunk for very long without the Universe getting wind of it.

# Wanting To Be Wanted

*My experience*

If ever there was a time when I cared about what people thought of me it was in high school. Anybody could devastate me just by saying something bad about me. I was like a puppet, and my strings were there for the pulling. Of course I tried not to let it show. I pretended to be "together," but unless everybody in the entire Universe loved me I felt like a failure. My mind chattered continuously about what I should have said that might have been better than what I actually said, what reaction others might have to my comments and behaviors, and what people really felt about me. I didn't think anyone was honest about the feelings they expressed towards me since I was so often dishonest about my feelings, pretending I liked everyone and nothing bothered me. I was anxious about everything, and the chattering in my mind never stopped. Never.

A friend once told me that when he was a little boy his teacher did a sociogram. She asked all the children to draw pictures of the desks in the classroom and place themselves where they wanted to sit, along with the names of the people next to whom they wished to be seated. Johnny recalled that every single child in the class wanted to sit next to him...except one. He said all he could think about was why that one kid didn't like him.

It didn't matter that every other child wanted Johnny as a neighbor; he was miserable thinking about the one child who didn't.

Johnny sounded just like me.

# My Path
# Not Yours

Going with someone you think is just about perfect except for that one measly little behavior that drives you to distraction? Like, maybe she drinks too much or he's really possessive?

You tell yourself there are so many other really great qualities about the person and you rationalize that nobody's perfect. You try to convince yourself that the characteristic you can't stand is no big deal.

STOP! It is a VERY big deal, and you know it deep down. Admit to yourself that this one quality that's potentially a deal-breaker isn't going to change. People don't change because you want them to; they change because they want to.

You can't MAKE someone want to change. If you've made it your mission to tweak or overhaul someone and it hasn't happened, go straight to your toolbox and get out the white flag. That's right; surrender. It's likely you're thinking you can change someone if he or she loves you enough, but as Tina Turner frequently sang, "What's love got to do with it?"

Nothing, Tina; zip, zilch, bupkis, nada and anything else that means love has nothing whatsoever to do with your honey changing that little, rapidly growing tumor of a problem that's a potential plague on your relationship. It's not going to happen unless he WANTS to change. If your honey du jour tells you he wants to make the changes you say are essential to moving forward in your relationship but doesn't actually DO it, cash in your chips and leave the casino; the odds are against you.

So, if for moral reasons you're a strict vegan who juices, eats wheatgrass and hangs out at health food stores, and you've found your perfect soul mate except for the itsy-bitsy problem that his idea of healthy eating is taking the skin off a knockwurst, you may have to wave the white flag before you find someone with whom you can do the happy dance after enjoying a romantic dinner of beansprouts and tofu.

# My Path, Not Yours
*my experience*

I loved being married. Isn't it great to find that special person you want to annoy for the rest of his life? LOL.

In this photo my late husband Richard is blowing out water the way he usually blew smoke rings.

Before we got married I asked Richard to stop smoking. In fact, I said I wouldn't marry him if he continued to smoke. I now know how ridiculous that ultimatum was. I also know he sneaked out to smoke for most of our fourteen year marriage.

Richard never ate a green vegetable during our entire relationship, nor did he eat fish, even if it was swimming in a sea of garlic butter. He lived on burgers, fries and soft drinks. He downed boxes of Mallomars at a single sitting, always accompanied by a quart or two of whole milk. Ahhh... but he worked out with weights, so he was able to convince himself he was healthy!

You can't believe the lengths to which I went in order to get Richard to care about his health and change his habits. I imposed on him everything from hypnosis to acupuncture to get him to stop smoking and eat healthy foods. I cooked fish balls and spaghetti, cheesecake with no sugar, no fat and no taste, but I kept trying. Of course, nothing worked. Even my eel soufflé wasn't the home run I thought it would be.

Eventually, the only realistic choice I had was to get out my white flag and surrender. I realized that my path, which by then included healthy living, was not Richard's path, so I stopped trying to change him, which freed me from a huge self-imposed burden. I decided to love him for who he was and not taint the time we had together by trying to control him.

It was difficult at first, but it became easier the more I practiced. Although we had much in common, I finally accepted the fact that we were from two different worlds ...at least!

# Comfort Zone

Consider this statement: "Life begins at the end of your comfort zone." You may have heard this before, but perhaps you didn't stop to think about it. It's one of those lines people use to justify their actions after they've done something uncharacteristic of themselves. Of course, everyone's comfort zone is different, so get the chalk out of your toolbox and draw the boundaries of your comfort zone. If you don't know what your boundaries are, how will you go beyond them? Draw the line between what you've already done and what you'd like to do if you didn't allow fear to stop you. That's your comfort zone.

Let's say your mother taught you to be afraid of everything except shopping, but once you start to pay the bills on your own the word *retail* makes you break out in a rash, so your comfort zone, which of course once included Bendel's and Nordstom's (before those previously selfless, philanthropic folks of yours turned vicious for no reason, and stopped footing the bills), now actually shrinks to include only thrift shops. When you stop crying, take out your chalk and draw a line between thrift shops and retail stores. Once you know what your comfort zone is, if you feel like living on the edge, you can extend it by darting right past your chalk line and heading for Bloomingdale's! That's what I mean about extending that comfort zone by just a little at a time.

Other examples include signing up for an adult education class, inviting someone you'd like to get to know to lunch or initiating small talk with a stranger while standing in line at the market. Maybe it's surfing, skydiving or swimming with sharks that extends your comfort zone.

The point is, any LITTLE STEP you take past your chalk line is a big step towards expanding the possibilities in your life. If you take a tiny step past your comfort zone every day the energy of your life will noticeably improve. It really works and you'll be proud of yourself for doing it. That's part of finding yourself. You'll be able to assess what works for you and what doesn't, but you have to stretch to see how you feel about something you've never done before. Maybe you'll love some of your new experiences and hate others, but it doesn't matter because you'll be living, feeling, learning. You'll be in the game!

Remember the turtle? He only made progress by sticking his neck out!

# Comfort Zone
*my experience*

In love, my comfort zone was well defined. He had to be someone I thought would never leave me. That really narrowed the field to those I didn't respect because they loved me when I didn't love myself, and those who were dependent on me.

What I ended up with were people who had issues up the wazoo and those who used me in one way or another, and I let that happen. It never occurred to me that what I was doing was setting myself up for one disaster after another. *Comfort Zone?* What was I thinking? I'd have been more comfortable standing next to the target at a shooting range!

Throughout my adult years I've been fortunate to have enough money on which to live well, so money didn't seem like a big issue for me. However, if I hadn't had enough money to satisfy my needs and didn't see any way out of that situation, I'm not so sure I wouldn't have narrowed my comfort zone to dating (or marrying) someone who did have more money than I. It's kind of like when a guy is well over six feet tall; he has no issues about being short (unless he aspires to become a jockey). Short men, on the other hand, frequently have serious hang-ups about their height. In other words, I give myself no credit (LOL) for not caring if someone had currency currently, because I had it, and could buy and do what I wanted. Some people thought I was to be admired for not caring if a boyfriend or husband had two nickels to rub together, but the truth is money mattered to me so much that I unconsciously but consistently chose men who had none so I could be in control! That said, I was only too happy to share money, trips, etc., with the people I chose, never even thinking they may have stayed for the goodies, like a lovely home, nice lifestyle and free everything.

It wasn't until I lost a fortune to two different boyfriends that I realized my success in staying in my comfort zone was instrumental in the failure of my romantic relationships. Once aware of this, I changed my comfort zone entirely.

I was terrified when I started dating Rich (not to be confused with Richard, my late husband), a gentle, kind, brilliant man with a sense of humor second to none, for whom I have the greatest respect. From our first date on, he insisted on paying for everything we did together. Allowing him to do so challenged me because I was out of my comfort zone and afraid. Since he was able to provide for himself, I was not in control of the relationship in the way I was used to, and had to believe I was worth staying with because of who I am, not for what I could provide to him. For me, the possibility of caring for Rich was an unnerving thought. I had to let go of my fear in order to be happy in love rather than unhappy in control.

In the immortal words of Mick Jagger, whose comfort zone stretches for miles in all directions, "It's alright to let yourself go as long as you let yourself come back."

# Teaching Others

Wouldn't it be great if you could just teach others how to treat you? Well, you already do!

Everything you do and say conveys to others what you expect from them. For example, let's say you're supposed to meet a friend for lunch at one o'clock and your pal doesn't show until one-thirty. If you don't express your annoyance to your friend and let it be known how unacceptable it is to keep you waiting for half an hour, you've taught that friend it's okay to keep you waiting. Does the name Pavlov ring a bell?

If you value your time, expect others to do the same. Sure unexpected events happen every so often and unforeseen circumstances can make people late, but that's when a phone call is important.

You might think, "I don't want to set a bad tone so I won't say anything." But NOT saying something sets a really bad tone because you'll feel hostile towards your friend and your negative energy will interfere not only with your lunch, but with your relationship. I've included the ABCs in your toolbox to remind you that how you act teaches people how you expect to be treated. YOU are the teacher, so if others repeatedly show disrespect for you it's because you've allowed it.

First ask your friend, "What kept you?" If the excuse is as unlikely as a pig in a sundress, express your feelings, get your annoyance or resentment out of the way, and then you can enjoy your lunch. You might say something like, "I'm glad to see you, although I have to tell you, I'm really annoyed that you kept me waiting for half an hour." CALMLY express your feelings and add that you'd have appreciated a phone call. Then ask your friend to be more considerate of your time in the future.

People often don't want to express their annoyances because they're afraid of sounding petty. But no feelings are petty; they're your feelings, and friendships are all about being vulnerable enough to share what hurts us as well as what makes us feel good. If you repeatedly have to say the same thing to someone, that friend isn't showing respect or consideration for you, and I suggest you rethink meeting him or her at designated times altogether. My guess is that someone who is continually inconsiderate of your time will be inconsiderate in other ways, too. In that case you may CHOOSE to be a full-time instructor, accept your DECISION to continue feeling upset and disrespected or phase out the relationship.

Sometimes you have to teach people that just because they show up before the party's over it doesn't mean they're on time.

# Teaching Others
*my experience*

Until recently, I had a close friend whom I'd met in college. Together, we'd been through everything from our children's births to our parents' deaths and every stage between. We'd been happy, sad and afraid together, and even though we blamed each other for our feelings of anger, hurt, betrayal or disappointment back in our twenties, we were brave and talked about our feelings. At first it was very scary to be so completely vulnerable, especially when we thought our grievances might seem petty. If we hadn't been willing to take those first risks, however, we'd never have learned that we COULD talk about everything. There were many times we said to each other, "I won't be treated this way." The more we grew and respected ourselves the more we gained respect from one another.

After decades of closeness our friendship ended when, after an argument, I reevaluated our relationship and decided it no longer was in my best interest to sustain it. She probably felt the same way, so we stopped talking and our friendship died. In this case it was time to part ways.

I don't believe a close friendship can sustain years of intimacy without disagreements, hostile feelings from time to time and honestly talking out issues. Little grievances build up over months and years. Have the courage to say, "Something's been bothering me and I want to clear it up because I don't want anything to get in the way of our friendship." Otherwise, you'll find yourself avoiding making that frequent call, not answering the person's message or just losing interest in the friendship altogether. You might not even know why you don't feel like seeing or talking to the person. The reason, however unconscious, will probably be the buildup of negative energy you harbor towards him or her.

By setting limits on what you're willing to tolerate you're teaching others how to treat you. When a friend repeatedly ignores your requests it may be time to wave goodbye, so get out the white flag and surrender. The Universe is trying to tell you something: it's unhealthy to hold on to a relationship that no longer is supportive or loving. Make room in your life for people who can not only teach you how to treat them, but those who can just as willingly learn from you what's acceptable to you and what isn't.

Remember, change is inevitable...except from a vending machine.

# Choices

Years ago New York Magazine did a study to determine why people wanted to live in New York City. Among the major reasons given were the theatre, opera, museums, ballet, and several other cultural or historically important venues. The researchers then asked the same people who'd cited these reasons how many times in the past five years they'd actually taken advantage of the activities or events to which they'd referred. About ninety percent of the respondents hadn't gone to even one of the places they'd checked as their reasons for living in Manhattan!

What does this mean? It means that we love choices. People feel secure, comfortable and happy knowing they have the OPPORTUNITY to take advantage of options, even if they never actually do.

Let's apply this finding to everyday life. Instead of telling your child or partner what he or she has to do, give choices. For instance, instead of saying, "Missy, this morning you have to iron my clothes, bring me breakfast in bed and stand on your head blowing dust bunnies off the floor" say, "Missy, which would you rather do first this morning: iron my clothes, bring me breakfast in bed or blow away dust bunnies?" When she answers you can give her the choice of what to do last.

Here's another example. Let's say you want to see a particular movie and your friend doesn't want to see it. Instead of arguing, you might say something like, "There are three movies I'm interested in seeing. In descending order they are: *The Bridezilla of Frankenstein, Driving Miss Crazy,* and *The Social Hairnet.* Which of these sounds best to you?" If he or she doesn't like any of your suggestions, ask your friend to give you some choices. The scale in your toolbox is included so you can weigh the possible alternatives to whatever you're considering. Just getting the scale out of the toolbox will buy you time to think, either about alternatives you want to offer someone (you may have to lend them your scale), or those you consider accepting.

Suppose you're a teenager and you want permission to go out on a weekday night, which you're not usually permitted to do. You could say to your parents, "I'd like to have special permission to go out one night this week. Would you prefer I go out on Monday, Wednesday or Thursday?"

I'm not guaranteeing you'll get the answer you want by providing choices, but I am saying you'll definitely improve your odds by offering choices instead of ultimatums. Whenever you tell people what they have to do you're more than likely to run into resistance. It's always good to offer alternatives. In fact, that's the only way you should do it!

So, do you think what I just said was enlightening, noteworthy or brilliant?

# Choices

*my experience*

A dear friend of mine gets stressed every time she has to make a decision. It doesn't matter if the choice is between tuna on rye or salami on a roll; anyone having lunch with her ought to expect to miss the six o'clock news.

Until I was in my forties, I too had a hard time making choices. My friend and I had both experienced fathers who always seemed to know the "correct" choices to make. Both of us were given few opportunities to make our own decisions about important matters in our lives. Because we had such strong, successful fathers, even as we got older we were only too happy to leave important decision making to our respective dads. Neither of us LEARNED to make good choices, not only because we weren't taught, but because we feared the consequences of being wrong, and therefore, relied on others to make choices for us. In rigid households "mistakes" are not well tolerated. For years we both suffered from CMDD (Choice-Making Deficiency Disorder).

When I did make choices the results proved to me that I was incapable of making good ones. For example, I let a "friend" use my credit card to rent a car, but he never returned the vehicle to the rental agency. It was eventually found in a wooded area and had been involved in a kidnapping! Naturally, I never heard from my so-called friend again. My father just shook his head and took care of whatever needed to be done to settle the rental car company's case against me. For seven years afterwards I was unable to get credit. All of this reinforced the idea that I should not make decisions on my own, that I was as dumb as a rock, and that my father didn't expect anything but lousy choices from me.

Following that episode and a few others in which I'd made poor decisions, it became part of our family lore that good decisions were not my forté. As a result, I continued to ask my dad to advise me when I had to make important choices, which he always did. Our conversations weren't over until I knew what decision HE thought I should make. Since I always went with my dad's choices I never explored alternative options, which limited me. Had I thought myself capable, I might have done some homework to find options my father hadn't considered. It would have helped me so much to make my own choices and live by the consequences without fearing that any decision that turned out to be disappointing would turn into a crucifixion.

My friend had a father who went berserk when she made a choice he thought was wrong. The repetition of his disapproval made a deep scar on her psyche. As an adult she had the impression there was a right and a wrong decision about everything. Because she expected to be wrong at least fifty percent of the time, she ruminated on every choice she had to make. Even buying lunch had the potential to be anxiety provoking because her mind paired all decision making with hazardous outcomes and parental criticism. For many parents good decisions are expected, and are therefore not praised; they come and go without fanfare and are easily forgotten. Decisions considered 'bad' on the other hand, are remembered, not necessarily because the decisions didn't get the desired results, but because of the consequences from parents (or other authority figures) who pre-determined that the decisions were wrong or bad, even before the results were known.

Who's to say what a bad choice is anyway? For every choice we make in life there's a lesson to be learned and a price to pay. That price may just be that you forfeit the other possibilities, but it's still a price. If you invest in a stock because you want financial security over the long term, you may not have the resources you need to take that vacation you want in the short term. If you choose a small college rather than a large one because you think you'd be uncomfortable as the proverbial little fish in the big pond, the price you pay may include fewer choices in the courses you take, a less prestigious staff of professors and a limited number of sports opportunities. If you go for the big school you could have large classes, get less personal attention and have so many tempting distractions that by the time you buy your Whatza Matta U sweatshirt you might discover you have the willpower of a hungry mouse on a tray of Gouda. Either way, there's always something you give up when you make a choice. Use your scale to weigh the value you place on what you think you'd get and what you think you'd give up for each choice you're considering.

There are ALWAYS unknowns for which you can't account. But if you've done your best and the outcome is not what you'd hoped it would be, consider that the Universe has other plans for you, and DECIDE to like whatever you get; you're going to have exactly the experiences you need in order for you to learn what you're here to learn. Always do your very best, and then TRUST THE UNIVERSE or whatever you call the Life Force, be it God, Jesus, Mohammed, Eternal Energy or something else. A rose by any other name is just as sweet as long as you put your trust in it.

If you decide to learn from every choice you make, there'll be no bad choices, just learning. That might be painful from time to time, but you'll be smarter and stronger for it. That kind of learning is part of life, and you'll grow and gain confidence from whatever decision you make. When you like the results you're pleased, and when you don't like them you learn valuable lessons you'll remember. You'll also realize that a choice resulting in an unfavorable outcome won't kill you. (Unless it's a VERY, VERY poor choice.)

As I said, fearful of making bad choices in my twenties, many times I acted on the decisions and experiences of my teachers and parents rather than using my own judgment. For example, whenever my friends and I went to singles bars I made choices based on the wise words of my mother: "Don't pick that up, you don't know where it's been."

# Being a Mirror

Here's an exercise that may surprise you. Try being a mirror. Act the way you'd like others to act towards you by pretending to be a mirror into which they're looking. In other words, if you'd like to see more people smiling at you, smile at them first.

Want to experience more generosity from people? Give more to them. Think others aren't listening to you? Listen to them very carefully. Want your kids or partner to give you greater respect? Let your mirror reflect respect back at you by first demonstrating your respect for them. Maybe your partner or your children have stopped showing you physical affection; no hand holding, hugs or little loving squeezes here and there. Be a mirror: grab a hand, give a hug and steal a squeeze. Let them see what that looks like again. Hold the mirror up to them until it reflects your own behavior right back at you.

It's so easy to blame other people for what we don't like in our lives, but blame is lame. Changing our own behavior is often all that's needed to produce the changes we've been struggling to see in others. The good news is that even though you can't change the wind you can always adjust your sails.

Don't give up on being a mirror before you've given the technique time to work. The odds are it will. Remember, it takes time to develop habits, so don't expect long-standing behaviors to unravel overnight. Persevere until you see the behaviors you'd like from others mirroring your own. If by some chance you're still trying on The Sixth Saturday in October, the worst that can happen is you'll know you gave it your best shot.

When you start to see big results from this little mirroring exercise, give yourself credit. It is, after all, a reflection on you.

# Being a Mirror

*my experience*

This is a photo of Jesse and his dad mirroring each other.

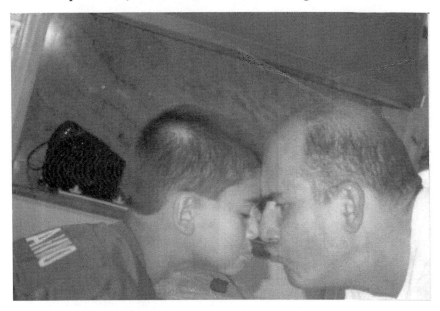

After a father commits suicide the chances of his son trying it go up about seventy percent. Following Richard's death Jesse tried to kill himself more than once.

We can expect our kids to do and say whatever we do and say. If we're nasty, they'll be nasty. If we show compassion for others, so will they. If we reach for alcohol to give us comfort, they will too. If we have no patience, scream, fight, throw tantrums, tell lies, put others down or put ourselves down, our kids will do exactly the same.

On the other hand, if we calmly treat challenges as a natural part of everyday life, stay calm, control our tempers, take our own time-out when we need it, exude self-confidence and kindness, have a positive attitude, show strength even in difficult times, and treat all our relationships with respect, so will our kids.

I was blown away this week when my daughter Nikki called from New York where she goes to school. She'd told her boyfriend how much she cared for him and he responded by saying she deserved someone who could feel the same way about her, and he thought it best they break up.

The following day she asked him to meet her for coffee and he agreed. She told him she wasn't trying to win him back, but that she needed closure and wanted to know specifically what prompted him to break up with her.

Apparently, he'd once experienced the pain of a broken heart when a previous girlfriend ended their relationship via e-mail. He never wanted to risk getting hurt like that again. He said that despite caring deeply for Nikki he couldn't bring himself to give one hundred percent of himself to anyone. He told her he loved everything about her and wanted to be able to give her all she deserved in life but couldn't because he was holding back.

In response, Nikki said she was going to talk to him as a friend, not a love interest. She expressed how genuinely sorry she felt for him and told him there can be no appreciation of the good without the bad. She reminded him that there are no guarantees in life and said if he wasn't willing to take risks he wouldn't grow or experience happiness regardless of the path he chose. Nikki said that despite the pain she was going through as a result of their break up she wouldn't change a single moment they'd spent together, and she told him that regardless of how much he cared for her she didn't want to be with someone who couldn't give of himself without reservation. She added, "I'm a pretty terrific person and I deserve someone who can give me one hundred percent."

I couldn't help but think how far she'd come from believing she wasn't deserving of happiness, and how far I'd been from feeling deserving of anything at nineteen.

The kicker came for me when she told me that throughout their conversation she kept thinking about what I'd taught her. "This was the payoff for all that breeding you gave me, Mom."

That was one of the high points of my parental experience. Still, I never think I look that good in the mirror.

I didn't even mention that her use of the word "breeding" was incorrect.

# Giving Advice

Do you think if people ask you for advice and you give it they're supposed to use your advice as the basis for the decisions they make? All they really want to know is what you think about their situation and what you'd do if you were in it.

Does someone you know refuse to give advice because those who asked for it didn't take it the last time they gave it? If that sounds like you, you've got to get over yourself! Frequently, when we ask for guidance we really just want to tell our story, but to make it more interesting to another person we ask for an opinion. Usually we don't realize that's what we're doing, but it may well be.

Uncertain about the appropriateness of various actions and reactions, people may ask six or seven others for advice, then act in a way they think is right for them, and that's a good decision.

If you're asked for guidance you'll need the blanket that's in your toolbox. When you give someone advice cover yourself by adding, "This is just my opinion, but you have to do what YOU feel is right." This way you remind yourself that the choice of what to do belongs to the advice-seeker not the advice-giver, and you disclaim any and all responsibility for the outcome.

Sometimes when we ask people for their advice we're really just looking for an accomplice.

# Giving Advice
*my experience*

My son Jesse recently moved to California. A few days ago he finally got the green light to move into an affordable apartment. Yesterday was moving day, and he phoned to say he found a used, cheap, queen-sized mattress on Craig's List but couldn't find anyone in his building to carry it up the five flights of stairs leading to his apartment. He was considering doing it himself or asking a friend to help him.

It's rare that I give advice to my children, but this was different. Jesse was experiencing a bout of Youngzheimer's Disease, the youthful equivalent of Alzheimer's. The poor kid apparently lost all memory of our frantic trips to the emergency room when his bad back suddenly disabled him.

I calmly (applause, applause) suggested that he call mattress stores and ask if there were any slightly soiled or older model mattresses in their warehouses. He said he'd done that but he couldn't afford the two hundred dollars a particular store wanted for a queen-sized mattress sample, even though the price included delivery!

What I wanted to say, or shriek, to be more precise, was something like, "Are you out of your freakin' mind? You'll spend one hundred bucks for a concert ticket but you can't afford two hundred for a mattress delivered to the door of your five story walk-up? You have a bad back, for God's sake!"

I didn't say it. (What we're going for here is progress, not perfection.) Instead I said, "Jesse, my brilliant child, I think the stress of moving may be clouding your judgment a little. When we hang up I'd like you to call the store and tell them to deliver the mattress tonight. 'There are two necessities in life: a good mattress and good shoes. Most of your life you're in one or the other.' " My good friend JP shared this gem of his mother's wisdom with me after she passed.

I'd sent Jesse off to L.A. with a decent amount of start-up money that I thought would last until he found a job. Certainly there was more than enough to buy a good mattress.

"This is a necessity Jesse," I advised.

"Thanks Mom, I'll do that right now," he said.

Was that really my Jesse? I could hardly believe this once oppositional, defiant boy had grown into a young man who was willing not only to listen to me, but to take my advice. Okay, so he also suffers from ISFBD (Intermittent-Shit-For-Brains Disorder), but what an improvement over being a juvenile delinquent!

Late in the day I phoned him to see how things were going. I said I had the feeling his earlier call was actually a request for advice.

"Of course," he said. "That's why I usually call."

Thank God I wasn't driving, because the shock of his statement would surely have caused a tree to hit me. (Just a little joke reference to taking responsibility.)

I'd always felt like a bad mother because I didn't have the energy to fight with my kids in order to get them to do things my way. I'd punished myself for my lack of nurturing since it seemed to me that compared to all the other moms I stayed out of my children's decision-making except when their safety was at stake. I was too depressed and tired to be as involved as the other parents and I didn't have the strength to argue about my children's decisions, even when I thought they weren't wise. I did, however, usually ask them what they thought they should do and encouraged them to name and understand the feelings behind their thoughts.

Consequently, today Jesse doesn't associate my giving advice with battles over control or with me trying to prevent him from growing up. All that guilt and it turns out I was doing the right thing, albeit for all the wrong reasons. Go figure! Parents, let this be a lesson to you. If you're a good enough parent to feel really guilty about what you're doing, you're probably doing a whole lot of good for your kids without even knowing it! I guess life really is like a box of chocolates: you never know what you're going to get, especially when it comes to raising kids.

From time to time Jesse apparently feels he'd like to have the benefit of my experience, so I ask what he thinks first, then I usually offer alternatives for him to consider. I know my children won't learn to make good decisions if I don't allow them to live by whatever decisions they make. This one, however, was health related, which is why I stepped in. Besides, pretty much my first thought was, one trip to the emergency room involves a co-pay that's more than the cost of the mattress!

## More of the Same Doesn't Work

Yesterday my friend and I were in an elevator rushing to get to an appointment. He knew we had to get off on the eighth floor, and you know how when you're in a hurry the elevator door seems like it takes forever to close? So impatiently, my friend kept hitting that eighth floor button...I mean, like seven times within about four seconds.

I commented to the other elevator occupant that we all seem to think that pushing the button more will move us along faster. He laughed and agreed, saying he does it all the time. I thought, *why do we push elevator buttons more and faster?* Obviously (in retrospect, of course), we don't want to feel powerless over anything. We want to believe we have some control over our world, so we do more of what doesn't work because we can't think of anything else to do!

It took but a moment for me to remember that everything happens for a reason. In many cases the Universe is giving us the message to slow down and smell the roses. This doesn't mean be passive. It means while you're waiting fill your time with a meaningful activity so you'll enjoy the wait. Count your blessings, chat with people, practice deep breathing or make up limericks in your head. (I can just hear my dad saying, "Where else would you make them up?") Learn the lesson. Slow down. Even enjoy the roadblocks you encounter in life. Ever think the roadblocks are there to force you to slow down? That's the time to get out the Yield sign and yield to the Universe.

Listen to what the Universe is saying. It's often telling us to enjoy our lives and be in the moment, which we can't do when we're focused on the future, as in trying to accomplish that which isn't ready to be accomplished. We'll get to the head of the line when we're supposed to, and we CAN control how happy or unhappy we are while we're waiting to get there.

Have you ever noticed that our patience isn't tested until we have none?

# More of the Same Doesn't Work

*my experience*

I'm sure you'll relate to this on some level, so now is the time to take the Yield sign out of your toolbox. If ever there was an example of the fact that more of the same doesn't work it was raising my children. When discipline didn't work I tried more discipline. When talking didn't work I talked more and louder. When ignoring their bad behavior didn't work I ignored them even more until I was off the charts for guilt. I took away privileges, toys and objects until the only thing left was a bronchial inhaler!

The problem was that the only way I knew how to behave when my kids acted like the annoying children they were was the same way my parents behaved when I annoyed them. It took quite a while for me to realize that what didn't work for my parents when they disciplined me wasn't going to work for me with my kids. Sometimes what seems natural isn't the best choice.

When I was growing up in the fifties and sixties, the way to have "good" kids was to discipline them, usually by taking something they wanted away from them until they succumbed. Pretty controlling, right?

Wait a minute. Children don't have to be controlled using punishment? Double duh.

Psychologist researchers have since proven that in the long run punishment doesn't work! I must have been busy searching the Web for some miracle cellulite cream when those flyers were handed out. How'd I miss that?

When my son stayed out all night I told him that if he did it again he wouldn't be allowed back in the house. A few weeks later, after yet another sleepless night with no call from Jesse, I was not about to back down. When he showed up at the door at two in the afternoon the following day he realized I had double locked all the doors so he couldn't get into the house. He stayed at his girlfriend's home for the next three months, during which time, he told me years later, he routinely used drugs and alcohol, stayed out all night and ate nothing but junk food...with the full awareness of his girlfriend's parents! I sure showed him a thing or two, didn't I?

He was only sixteen at the time, and I have to admit that after Richard's suicide I was relieved to be free of the constant strain of Jesse's unpredictable, often frightening behavior. I thought I had done all I could to help Jesse, when in retrospect, all I did was criticize him under the guise of wanting him to be a more conscientious, more productive child. I was angry with Richard for putting the kids and me in our situation, and I sometimes unwittingly took it out on Jesse, whose looks and behavior were increasingly similar to his dad's.

I'm sorry to say that when it came to my children I did more talking than listening. I tried to rationalize lecturing instead of listening, but the only excuse I could think of was that under the law of gravity it takes more energy to shut one's mouth than to open it. Even I couldn't bring myself to accept such a lame rationalization. I have standards!

When the light bulb finally went on I made a conscious CHOICE to raise my kids the way I thought was best. Believe it or not, up until that point it seemed to me there were only two ways to raise children: the right way and the wrong way. I sure didn't want to do it the wrong way. Certainly not while my parents were alive!

I finally decided to understand my children. There were many raised eyebrows when I didn't punish my kids for their misbehavior. The concept of not punishing the little darlings as a first line of defense against losing parental control is frightening to many parents.

For example, I stopped making threats and saying things like, "I forbid you" when my son said he hated school and wanted to drop out. Instead, I started to make statements like, "That must really suck. What makes you hate it? What would you do if you dropped out?" I asked non-threatening questions until I learned enough to see things from his point-of-view. Then I put myself in his shoes. (Did I mention the smell?)

Guess what happened when I stopped acting like I thought a parent was supposed to act and started being a compassionate, loving person to Jesse? He started...ARE YOU READY FOR THIS???... talking to me!! As a result, he felt I genuinely wanted to know about his feelings, and he started noticing that I was taking them into consideration when I made decisions concerning him. Instead of using substances to kill his feelings he began acknowledging them to himself and to me. The more our relationship changed and the more Jesse matured, the more I shared my own emotions with respect to shame, guilt, disappointment, fear and love. Soon, and until this very day at the age of twenty-three, Jesse and I talk openly and without judgment (...except when we don't). Of course, some things are off limits because it wouldn't be appropriate for either of us to be privy to the private intimate details of the other's life.

While my daughter was constantly reminded about the dangers of drugs and alcohol, all my talking fell on deaf ears. One day when Nikki was about sixteen I was entertaining some people in our living room when she came home from an afternoon at the beach with her friends. Nikki said a quick hello to everyone and headed for her room. About fifteen minutes later I went in to check on her. She was fast asleep. When I bent down to kiss her cheek I could smell alcohol on her breath. My thought, which immediately followed the one where I strung her up by her eyelashes, was to punish her, which I did. In retrospect, it seems as though I was determined to expend the most energy to get the least desirable results possible.

Surprise, surprise! Punishment didn't work! I finally sat down with her and talked very candidly about my own earlier substance abuse and how I used drugs to prevent me from experiencing painful feelings of inadequacy and guilt. I told her I could completely understand why she wanted to shut out certain things, like her dad's suicide. It was she who then said, "Yeah, but the only problem is it doesn't work because I just end up with a headache and the hurt is still there."

All I could do was hold her and tell her how sorry I was. For the first time, I didn't feel inadequate because I couldn't "fix" her sorrow. She began to open up about her feelings and agreed to see a psychologist. Nikki will be twenty-one in December, and today she and I are like fruit and fiber; we can make a go of it no matter what! She can even joke about some of her dad's endearing idiosyncrasies and speak of him lovingly, without hurting.

Among the many lessons I learned from this experience is that the best way to get kids to do anything is to forbid them to do it.

# PART THREE

### Your Mission, Should You Decide To Accept It...

1. Use words to express how you feel
2. Move on if people dislike you
3. Accept others without trying to change them
4. Stay green and grow
5. Train people to treat you well by showing respect for yourself
6. Give choices not ultimatums
7. Be the image you want reflected back at you
8. Only give advice with a caveat
9. If it's broke fix it by changing your approach

# Part Four:
## On Love
These are my uber-tools to add to your magical box:

1.  **STRING:** to tie around your finger so you'll remember to do thoughtful deeds daily

2.  **ONE DOZEN RED ROSES:** to remind you to be kind to yourself

3.  **BRAIN:** labeled Inner Genius so you don't follow advice of your Inner Moron

4. **EARPLUGS:** to prevent you from relying on what people say rather than what they do

5. **NOTEBOOK:** to keep a record of what your loved ones enjoy

6. **CALCULATOR:** to track ratios in relationships

7. **SHOVEL:** to scoop away any crap you've left behind

8. **BOX OF CRAYONS:** to create beautiful memories of people you want to remember

9. **SCRAPBOOK:** to share good memories of those who've passed

# That Old Feeling

When I was in my early teens and dinosaurs roamed the earth, a guy named Johnny Mathis sang a song with the lyrics, "It's not just for what you are yourself that I love you as I do, but for what I am when I am with you."

That is so profound.

Remember when you first fell in love? You felt like a million bucks, right? That's because the person you loved also loved you, and treated you like royalty. You came to see yourself through that person's loving eyes, and through those eyes you were amazing, gorgeous, thoughtful, sweet, funny, and entirely fabuloso.

Part of what you loved was feeling like you WERE the great person your partner believed you to be.

You know what happens after a while. People start taking each other for granted.

After a decade and a couple of kids you can't automatically expect your partner to ping your every pong. So if you want to feel more of what you used to feel, you've got to do more of what you used to do!

Tell your partner some of the qualities you like about him or her. Expressing appreciation for your partner will go a long way towards being a mirror of love. You might, for example, tell your guy how much you admire his ability to make and keep friends, or you could tell your girlfriend you love her open-mindedness. If you want your relationship to be hot again, comment positively on the specific things your partner does. A simple, "I appreciate it when you do the dishes" or, "I love the fact that you drive and let me sit back and relax" is all it will take for your honey to begin looking for ways to praise you.

If you're at a point in your relationship where the nicest thing you can say is, "Gee Eddie, you sure know how to swirl a snifter," say it! Don't expect your partner to immediately respond to just one appreciative comment with another directed towards you, however. Find the string in your toolbox and tie it around your finger to remind you to do and say nice things frequently. Really, do it. In time your partner will reciprocate. However, if by some chance it doesn't happen by the Twelfth of Never, put on your track shoes.

The poet Robert Frost said, "Love is an irresistible desire to be irresistibly desired." To take a step in that direction you have to remind your sweetie, and maybe even yourself, that he or she is still special to you and continues to be appreciated. I don't know about you, but when I find out someone thinks I'm the greatest thing since the push-up bra, I'm automatically drawn to that person and in his or her presence I feel particularly good. It's pretty much universal that we like those who like us. Ignoring your partner's positive effect on your life because of pent up hurts or resentments will keep your relationship spiraling downward. Be a mirror of the love you want to receive.

If you want the whole enchilada you've got to bring the cheese.

# That Old Feeling

*my experience*

I adore this photo because the love between these two people jumps out at you, doesn't it?

Scientists tell us that the feelings portrayed in this picture generally last for about eighteen months, give or take a few. Our bodies and minds can't sustain the intensity of new love forever. Think about it. You'd never get anything done!

After about eighteen to twenty-four months of slobbering all over each other the chemical oxytocin (Pitocin) kicks in. It's the same chemical a woman's body emits when her baby is born, and it's frequently called the cuddling hormone because it causes new moms to want to bond with (cuddle) their babies. In romantic relationships when this hormone is produced, couples often start to lose the high degree of excitement they had in the beginning stages of their relationships. They might, for example, stop going to clubs as much as they once did and prefer to snuggle up on the sofa and watch movies together. Oxytocin has a sort of anti-stimulating effect by lowering the cortisol levels that raise blood pressure and produce stress.

That does NOT mean, as B.B. King once sang, "The Thrill is Gone," although I used to think that's exactly what it meant. In those days my attention span was about ten seconds and eight of them had to be a compliment! My mother could always tell when I was getting close to bolting from a relationship and she'd ask me, "Who's on deck?" More often than not I already had my eye on someone because I was chasing the thrill of new love.

As soon as the initial rush was gone I'd leave one boyfriend and go on to the next. The Universe was simply telling me I should stop twirling about in the whirlwind I was in and get back to normal life, but I hadn't yet learned its language, so I misunderstood the message it was sending me via my feelings. The thrill wasn't gone; it's just that I had to be WILLING to be thrilled by different aspects of the relationship as time went by.

The initial rush of attraction changes with time.

The key to love after your eyes are no longer glazed over and your feet touch the ground again, is expressing the same kind of appreciation, adoration and gratitude you expressed in the beginning of your relationship.

In the words of the great theologian, Martin Buber, "You love the love that loves you." All you have to do is show it.

You go first.

# Love Thyself

Yesterday I happened to be in a car dealership and the salesman, who had been watching my interaction with my honey said, "You two look so happy. I can't seem to find anyone to make me happy. Why is that, Dr. Howard?"

"You just said it," I replied. "You have to BE happy BEFORE you find someone."

In over twenty years of counseling couples and love-seekers I have repeatedly seen that if you're not happy with yourself, you don't have a shot at being happy with anyone. Oh, it's not that you won't feel the thrill of a new love for a while when Mr. or Ms. Close Enough comes into your life. But think about it; if you can't sustain happiness by yourself, how will you suddenly get it from someone else? Have you ever been in such a relationship for a prolonged length of time where you thought your partner would *make you happy* and found that your neediness, jealousy and possessiveness did NOT get in the way? For how long were you genuinely happy? Tell the truth and don't consider only the good times. (If someone just broke up with you, you probably believe that the one who got away made you happy. Get real. You broke up, so how good was the relationship and how happy were you?)

A happy, healthy person, capable of having a good relationship with you is someone who's happy without a partner and CHOOSES to be in a relationship, but doesn't NEED to be.

Phrases like "Love Thyself" are so overused they seem to have lost their impact. We've habituated to them, so they aren't as meaningful as they once were. But that particular phrase is THE KEY to your happiness. That's why I put the dozen roses in your toolbox; to remind you to act lovingly towards yourself by showing respect for your health, your feelings and your time. Saying *no* when you don't want to do something, extending your comfort zone and calmly and appropriately expressing feelings are some examples of honoring and respecting yourself.

The old time comic Groucho Marx once said he didn't want to be a member of any club that would have him. Can you really respect someone who loves you if you don't love and respect yourself?

# Love Thyself
*my experience*

I met Richard, AKA husband number three, in a Twelve-Step Program in New York City when I was in recovery from addictions. He'd dropped out of college where the closest he ever got to a 4.0 was his blood alcohol level. You know the saying, "If life hands you lemons make lemonade"? I guess life handed Richard tomatoes because he made Bloody Marys! Richard had been in the Program for a while and when we met he was an inspiration to me. I'd stopped using drugs for many reasons, not the least of which was that I was nearly thirty-seven years old and got the same feeling from standing up too fast!

What impressed me about Richard was his dedication to his own well-being. His commitment to sobriety reflected a determination to be someone he could respect and love. He had specific goals which, on a daily basis, included going to a gym, working hard at his job, talking to his sponsor, working the Twelve Steps and staying sober. When he shared at meetings it was obvious that he was working diligently towards loving himself. It was as though he sent roses to himself every day because he knew he was worth it.

In those days Richard was able to resist using drugs and alcohol because he followed a plan that kept him busy with positive activities and connected him to people who wanted him to succeed. After meetings he often went out for coffee with the many friends he'd made at daily meetings. They gave Richard the positive reinforcement that helped him see he was moving towards his goals.

When I first stopped using drugs I had no idea how to begin loving myself. I threw away my Lilly of the Valium perfume and observed Richard doing what he needed to do to like himself minute by minute, hour by hour, day by day. He checked in with himself several times each day to make sure he was on the right track in both his thoughts and behaviors. He was actually CREATING the Self and the life he consciously wanted. The more he worked at it the more self-respect he developed and the more others wanted to be around him. As the weeks passed he exuded positive energy that arose from his increasing strength and sense of completeness.

Richard was on his path. When I asked him out he declined, saying I needed to do work on myself before I started dating him. He said he'd come too far to put himself in jeopardy by getting involved with a newcomer; it would be easy for him to get off track if he entered into a relationship before he was ready. In addition, he didn't want me to compromise my newfound sobriety by focusing on a distraction: him. Even though I was being shot down, I liked him for it. He was solid, and I knew I wanted a relationship with him.

We both knew he was worth the wait.

# Love and Your Inner Genius

I believe completely in trusting your gut feelings and listening to your inner genius; that is, unless you're so madly in love that you can't think of a single imperfection in your fantasy person. When that's the case, you can't think at all. Love like this happens when two people who are mutually attracted don't know each other! Apparently, that's when your inner genius takes a flying leap out the window and doesn't come back until the cobwebs in your brain are gone. Go directly to your toolbox and you'll see a brain labeled "Inner Genius." That's the tool you need if you relate to this. Keep it with you at all times, especially if you're prone to confusing fantasy with reality, because this isn't love and you aren't in a Lifetime movie. The media fuels this fantasy, and if you confuse it with love it can result in serious depression.

That's why I'm now going to speak to your inner moron. Don't believe your own made up story about a love interest you barely know or get hooked on the superficial appearances of Ken or Barbie look-alikes. Make the DECISION to love someone based on characteristics that will sustain you, like honesty and thoughtfulness. The high of fantasy love feels great, but you'll need a crash helmet if you choose this path. In case you haven't seen the sign above the red flag where your fantasy person is standing, it reads, *The higher the high, the harder the crash.*

Fantasyland is a great place to visit, but don't expect to live there. Have a little reality chat with your inner moron before you start doodling your names together.

# Love and Your Inner Genius

*my experience*

Here I am at the tender age of twenty-one with Tommy, my first husband. Ahh, I was so mature in those days...I married him because he locked himself in a hotel room and said he would do himself in if I didn't tie the knot.

You mean that's NOT a good reason to get married?

At twenty-one I was at a point in my life that all I wanted was a swag light and a husband. Tommy was completely unpredictable and flamboyant, and if that isn't the recipe for a great marriage, he also looked like the guy on the TV show *Chips*. How could I resist an unpredictable, flamboyant fellow who looked like Chips and threatened to kill himself out of love for me?

DUH! How could I NOT have seen what a blind schnauzer would have seen?

Well, there was also a big ring involved and it sort of... ummm...uh, blinded me, if you catch my drift. I was in love with the whole idea of being married to someone who bought drinks for everyone on the plane, lived impulsively, and managed our finances with the precision of a leaf blower. It never once occurred to me that he'd probably inherited his mother's bipolar disorder.

Did I for a moment suspect that any of the traits I loved were potential problems? Nahhhhh. I wanted a wedding!

It's so easy to be unconscious. When we want what we want when we want it, when our hormones scream out for recognition and we answer faster than a cheetah with a hotfoot, when we refuse to pay attention to our lives and aren't honest with ourselves, we get a marriage like I had: one that ends.

# Believe Actions,
# Not Words

Don't believe everything you hear. In fact, get the earplugs out of your toolbox and make sure they fit snugly; you don't want what you hear people say to determine what you believe about them. Watch what they DO rather than listening to what they say. When people's actions aren't in sync with their words, believe their actions, not their words.

If you're looking for love, and most of us are at one time or another, be aware that you WANT to believe what your adorable love interest tells you. But first and foremost, PAY ATTENTION to the person's ACTIONS, not his or her words.

For example, if a guy tells you he values honesty above all else, but you overhear him giving a made-up excuse to someone about why he was late for an appointment, believe the dishonest excuse behavior, not his lovely words to you. Words and deeds have to match.

Let's say you try to be supportive when your son (or daughter) comes home to show you his spanking new tattoo of Rambo with a sword stuck in his chest and blood dripping all the way down to the No Tattoo Zone. (One can only hope there is one.) When your throat opens up, you make some complimentary remarks about the artistry and colors. Even if you deserve a statuette for your performance, do you think your little darling will believe what you've said after he sees you stick your head in the oven?

I think not. Unfortunately, most situations where people aren't honest are a tad more difficult to read.

What I'm trying to say is that if a girl claims to be ultra thoughtful to others but you notice she lacks consideration for her parents or friends, pay attention to what she does rather than what she says. And don't believe anyone who tries to convince you her dishonesty or misrepresentation was an isolated instance. When it comes to honesty, there's no such thing.

We all WANT to believe he or she is our Magical One, but when you get the tingles don't make excuses for people whose actions don't seem to match their words. If you do, that tingle you feel today may be a full-blown rash by tomorrow.

# Believe Actions, Not Words

*my experience*

This lesson was difficult and painful for me. I always assumed I should start out taking people at their word even though the Universe tried to teach me over and over again that trust has to be earned. Why did I have to be taught the same lesson so many times? Because I WANTED to believe that the people I dated were who they said they were. I finally learned that a man isn't honest just because he's never had the opportunity to rob a bank.

When we want to believe someone because doing so fulfills some hope we have, we're often blind to the truth. Once we believe someone or something, it takes monumental evidence to change our minds. The disparity between what we believe and what we experience is called cognitive dissonance. Our brains don't like these contradictions. They try to make the two compatible, and in so doing we select the one we like best and ignore the other. That's one reason it's difficult to acknowledge someone's disgusting behavior once we think of him or her as THE ONE. By overlooking the contradiction our brains aren't confused. In my case, I liked what I heard and believed a whole lot more than what I saw, so I pretty much ignored my actual experience and went with my high hopes and fantasies.

I lived with a man for over three years, and despite every indication that he was a phony, I supported and defended him. Why was it so difficult to see what was right in front of me? Because he gushed over my "talents," telling me all the things I wanted to hear. According to his words I was the most creative person he'd ever met, the most stunning woman he'd ever seen and undeniably the smartest being on earth. Since I wanted so badly to believe he was telling the truth about me, I had to believe he was honest! After all, if I had recognized his innate dishonesty I would've had to question the validity of what he said about me. It was this experience that taught me I needed to go out and get earplugs, and I'm thrilled to give you some to put in your toolbox.

I'm embarrassed to say that although the man I'm talking about is actually a sociopathic liar, with all my training I couldn't see it. I mean, everyone has a right to be stupid, but I was really taking advantage!

Looking back, his dishonesty was as obvious as the nose on his face, which by the way, wasn't real either!

# Bonding Made Easy

Doesn't it feel great when a friend remembers your birthday or someone brings you the special banana nut bread you love or sends you a scarf in the eggplant color you once mentioned is your favorite? Acts of kindness and love like these make us feel special and bond us to the people thoughtful enough to remember what makes us happy.

One way to start building your self-esteem is to begin gathering information about what brings enjoyment to the people you like. The notebook in your toolbox is there for just this purpose. If you don't want to carry around a notebook you can keep notes on your computer or in your daily planner. It's the notes you keep that matter, not where you keep them. You just have to remember to look at them and DO something to let those you love know they're important to you.

You might call a special friend and tell her about a movie that touches on a topic close to her heart, or you could send her the movie trailer by e-mail. Stick a little note in someone's jacket pocket or lunchbox saying you'll have a favorite snack ready when he or she gets home. Let your brother know you're thinking of him by sending him articles about topics near and dear to him. It will show him he's important to you. When you do nice things for other people without expecting a "payoff," you like yourself more.

It's not about what you buy for people or even how much time you spend with them. The thoughtful gestures I'm referring to here are different. They're about making something important to you because that something is important to a person you care about.

Can you mention five things your sweetie really enjoys? How about your kids or your parents? If you can't think of five little trinkets, songs, articles or something else that would bring a smile to the faces of those you love, consider making a conscious DECISION to notice what they like. Put the notes you take in writing and look at them each week. Small acts of thoughtfulness will improve your relationships even if they're already good. Just one act of kindness each week will add much positive energy to your life and make you feel like you're a kind and thoughtful person. This is exactly the kind of gesture that gives you pride in who you are and helps you feel great.

I remember once when I was doing marital therapy, a client complained that her husband didn't know one single thing she liked. "That's absolutely not true," he said.

"Really?" she asked, "What's my favorite flower?"

Her eyes nearly rolled out of her head when he replied, "Pillsbury?"

# Bonding Made Easy
*my experience*

Several months ago my significant other happened to mention that he loved rack of lamb. He spoke of how his mom used to make it and said the smell of it brought back wonderful memories.

I rarely eat meat (rare or otherwise), but I picked up a rack of lamb at the market and found a recipe that looked good. One weekday evening I invited him to dinner and served the lamb. The dinner was great and he was very appreciative.

About three months later, during a discussion we were having about ways to express love and appreciation, he spoke of the rack of lamb dinner. He said it was one of the most caring things I could have done for him. The fact that I remembered how much he loves lamb SHOWED HIM that he was important to me, and preparing it for him on an otherwise ordinary weekday night was a bonus. Naturally, I ran out in search of a notebook for my toolbox as fast as my little legs could carry me and began taking notes. I hope you'll put yours to good use. The one pictured is ordinary, but the one in your toolbox has an outrageous cover. But I digress...

I was surprised that such a small act meant so much to him. He said that no gift or declaration of affection could convince him of my feelings for him as much as my acting on something he'd said in passing.

All you have to do to make bonding easy is to first watch and listen carefully for clues to what someone enjoys, and second, act on those clues by DOING something that shows you cared enough to notice and remember.

Talk is cheap. Rack of lamb...not so much.

# The Ratio

Ever hear of the "One to Eleven Rule"? It seems that couples with the best odds of staying together are those whose ratio of positive to negative comments or deeds is at least one to eleven. According to a well-known study, EVERYTHING you and your honey do in your relationship can be rated as a plus or a minus. That means for every eleven negative things you do, if you want your odds of staying together to increase, you'll need to do or say at least one thing that's positive. You might not agree with the researchers that certain behaviors are negative, but that's because they've become so incorporated into your general style and attitude towards your partner that you just accept them as neutral. Examples of such behaviors might be rolling your eyes when, for the six hundredth time, your guy talks about the vacation to Bali he's going to take you on as soon as he once again fits into his Coast Guard uniform, or when you don't look up from your newspaper after your sweetie pie says she's thinking of shaving one side of her head and getting a discreet Black Sabbath tattoo on it. Call them sticklers, but those kooky psychologist researchers consider the eye rolling and indifference negatives!

Since I barely made it through high school math I put a calculator in my toolbox, not to keep a running count, but to remind me that ratio is important. I slipped one into your toolbox for the same reason.

Here are some more examples of pluses and minuses:

"How could you possibly not know where the butter is?" That's a negative, and so is, "Sweetie, you're dribbling," especially if it's said loudly in a quiet restaurant. A positive gesture might be a gentle touch on your partner's shoulder when you enter the room or leaving a Mercedes with your honey's name on the license plate parked where the '78 Cordoba used to be. You get the idea.

So increase the positives, reduce the negatives, and notice the amazing effect that change has on your relationship.

And remember...don't sweat the petty things.

Don't pet the sweaty things either.

# The Ratio

*my experience*

My brother Bob and I threw a fantastic bash for our parents on the occasion of their fiftieth wedding anniversary. When I look at this picture of my parents taken at the celebration, I'm amazed these two people stayed together for over fifty years. In their day few people knew any of the "rules" about how to communicate. My brother and I may have heard our folks argue once or twice, but I think they just stuffed most of their feelings and remained silent. My father probably thought if my mother wanted a communicator she should have married Walter Cronkite.

I can't say I recall my parents giving each other many compliments, encouraging each other or praising one another very often. Everything from dinner to gardening was expected to be of the highest standards, and if it wasn't there was criticism. When all a person hears is criticism, he or she soon feels defeated and hopeless. Over time, hopelessness leads to depression.

When my brother Bob and I grew up and went out on our own and our dad retired, I'm sure a great deal of pressure was off our folks' shoulders. They were increasingly relaxed, spent more quality time together and grew closer. Still, I wish I had seen or heard them express greater appreciation for one another while Bob and I were growing up. It's ironic that in times of greatest stress many couples seem to separately go inward and become self-absorbed when their greatest strengths could be in expressions of love and support for one another.

It's been my experience that couples have to show each other appreciation and recognition on a consistent basis, preferably several times each day, in order for their relationships to THRIVE, not just survive. In the course of daily life there are so many details and routines, so many disappointments and challenges, so much to accomplish and cross off the list, that it's easy to forget to express gratitude for a partner's contributions to our lives. Most of us think only of what WE give to our relationships.

We all want to be told we're doing a great job, making a difference, and that we're appreciated for just being who we are. Saying "I love you" isn't sufficient. Those three little words become meaningless if ACTIONS don't back them up. We can't say "I love you" once or twice a day, then criticize, scowl or remain emotionally distant the rest of the time. If we do, our children grow up confused, expecting love and criticism to go together. It's a mixed message, kind of like saying, "I love the way you look in purple; it really brings out the veins in your legs."

We sometimes wonder why people stay with partners who are constantly critical of their mates and put them down at every opportunity. Often, these are people who've grown up in homes in which criticism became linked to love.

Of course it's okay to overlook little slights in an otherwise harmonious relationship wherein acts of kindness and good intentions are mutual. Part of the job of each partner, however, is to consciously balance those slights by looking for and finding attributes and actions to appreciate. Expressing gratitude is like putting money in a savings account; it gives us a nice balance and helps both partners feel secure.

Keep the One to Eleven Rule in mind and DECIDE to act on it each day. You'll both be amazed at the interest you accrue.

# Internet Dating

Hello there daring Internet daters! Listen carefully, please.

Do not put the best picture you've ever taken in your entire life, from 1967, on your profile. If you decide to go out with someone your date will eventually see you, duh, and you'll be considered an immediate disappointment, and a dishonest one at that. You know that big ol' shovel in your toolbox? I included it so you can shovel away all the crap you may be putting out there. Ladies, if you say you look like Sandra Bullock but more closely resemble Sandra's buttocks, or if your profile states that people think you look like Samantha from *Sex and the City*, but you actually look like a llama's mama, you'll be speed-dating at the speed of light, but not by your choice.

Be honest about who you are and your likes and dislikes, and be clear about what is and isn't acceptable to you.

Be creative though. Everybody wants someone who sizzles like bacon, has a sense of humor like Jerry Seinfeld and an I.Q. higher than a toilet seat. So write specifics...but unless you're willing to be arrested by the cliché police, not the one about walking barefoot on the beach in the moonlight...yawn, yawn.

If seeing your great big family on Sundays is very important to you, say that! If your child, pet cobra or chimpanzee is the current love of your life, say that too. Sure you'll lose some potential repliers, but aren't you trying to screen out those whom you wouldn't consider serious contenders for a place in your life and heart?

One additional warning: unless you're sending out free Pepto-Bismol to everyone on the dating site, do not reference your monumental wealth, even a little. It's sickening! I know it's tempting to try to use whatever you can to generate responses, but if you let your money do the talking your relationship won't have real value. You want a partner who's going to hold your hand even if he or she doesn't know about the 24 Karat Rolex Collection you've stashed in the sixth bedroom of your world-renowned yacht, "The Braggart."

Remember, money isn't everything. In fact, after taxes it isn't anything!

I love Albert Einstein's quote: "Not everything that counts can be counted, and not everything that can be counted counts."

Why didn't I think of that?

# Internet Dating

*my experience*

About three years after the suicide of my husband I joined an Internet Dating Service. I thought it would be a good way to slowly make contact with men again. I figured I could write to them and maybe even chat on the phone with them for months before meeting face to face.

I decided to be precise and honest about what I wanted and was clear that I needed to be one hundred percent myself right from the start. I was tired and didn't have the emotional or physical fortitude to go out of my way to look great or be "on" all the time. Anyway, it's hard to be on when you're always a little off!

I dyed my hair bright red and cut it to about an inch from my scalp because I thought it would give me a new lease on life. It actually did. I felt young and sexy for the first time in years.

Instead of writing my profile I decided to explain myself in a poem. One of the verses was:

I don't care at all if you're fat, bald or thin;
The beauty I'm seeking comes from within.

As a result of those lines men of all shapes and sizes, most of whom appreciated my values, contacted me. I greatly increased my opportunities to meet people with whom I could form friendships that might evolve into romantic relationships. A former male model wrote that it was great to know there was someone who didn't just care about his looks. (I never care about how someone else looks; I only care about how I look.) My poem also said:

> Want a body that's twenty? That wouldn't be me;
> I'm no Demi Moore, but then neither is she.

I was honest about myself. It's so much better than being rejected when the truth comes out after you meet. I'd rather under-promise and over-deliver than over-promise and under-deliver. Nevertheless, I've heard so many horror stories about people misrepresenting themselves on dating sites that I couldn't sleep at night if I didn't include a shovel in your toolbox. (Don't be insulted; I put it in everyone's.)

It's not that you shouldn't put your best foot forward. But guys, don't put it forward in shiny wingtips if you really only wear sneakers.

And ladies, don't put it forward in four-inch heels, a dress so tight you look like a sausage and enough make-up to be mistaken for a Japanese Kabuki. If you do, he or she may be excited by how you look at first, but after seeing you au natural at the gym, you may no longer have reason to brush the confetti out of your Spanx.

# Stayin' Alive

At various times people have told me they were afraid to stop mourning for someone who passed because they thought if they did so the person's memory would fade. While mourning may keep the memory of a loved one from fading, it erodes the mourner's ability to feel joy and happiness. It's far better to keep someone's spirit alive by celebrating his or her life than it is to continue mourning that person's death.

You can honor people who have transitioned by thinking of what those people did that contributed to your life, like the lessons you learned from your interactions with them, the values and fun they brought to your experiences, the way they influenced you and how you may have influenced them. You want to remember the happiness they brought to your life, not the pain you feel at their loss.

Even after they've passed, you can actually make the lives of those who've crossed over more meaningful. Sharing with others your favorite stories, showing pictures, explaining how these people expressed their feelings, talking about the influence they had on the community and anything else of an interpersonal nature will keep loved ones close to you. These are ways you can actually *introduce* someone who passed to someone who never even met the deceased.

It's not unusual for people to say they "talk" to their moms and dads after their parents have transitioned. If someone to whom you were close has passed, you can probably "hear" what that person would say to you if, for example, you asked, "What advice can you give me about...?"

First picture the person standing in front of you. See what clothes she's wearing, what her hair looks like and how she's standing. Out loud, ask whatever you want. You'll "hear" the response if you sit quietly and listen. These spirits live with you. They've shared their energy and it's become part of who you are. You won't lose them. You can't lose them. Their energy remains after their hearts stop beating. Paying attention to that energy keeps them within your reach. The more you practice "meeting" them, the more you'll feel their energy.

During our time in this realm, in order to interact with loved ones we have to call, visit or communicate electronically. After we lose our bodies our spirits are accessible to those who love us 24/7.

I sure hope that when it's time for me to exit the planet the people who love me will use their crayons to color my life beautifully. Don't you wish the same for you and your loved ones?

# Stayin' Alive
*my experience*

One way to keep people's spirits alive after they've passed is to share their stories and wisdom with others. My dad passed years ago, but he continues to help people because I've shared his wisdom with friends and clients many times, and the sharing helped them as it did me. This is where I use my crayons, so take note.

By my early thirties I'd earned a couple of academic degrees and was teaching English. What I really wanted, however, was to become a psychologist, but I was overwhelmed by the amount of time and work it would take for me to achieve that goal.

I said, "Dad, it's going to take nine more years for me to become a psychologist, and by that time I'll be forty!" To which my father replied, "And how old will you be in nine years if you don't become a psychologist?"

He folded up my list of course requirements and instructed me never to look at it again.

"What exactly is it that you have to do *today*?" he asked.

"Get the application," I said.

"Great. That's all you have to do today. Tomorrow you can fill it out, and each day you'll look only at what has to be done that day. If you do that, you'll be forty in nine years and you'll have a Ph.D. in psychology."

And that's what I did. I love the colors in that picture.

We are here and it is now. What a relief it is to stay in the moment.

Thanks, Dad.

# Creating Good Memories

Do you remember events from your early years the same way your parents or siblings do? I treated someone who often spoke of being forbidden to sit on the white sofa in his family's living room while he was growing up. That rule became a metaphor for the rigidity of his parents who, as he recalled, were more concerned with appearances than comfort. We tagged certain experiences "the white sofa" to represent how stifled he felt growing up. One day, at my client's request, I had the opportunity to speak with his mother about her son's feelings regarding his childhood. The conversation went like this:

"Can you tell me about the white sofa?"

"What white sofa?"

"The one you had in your living room when your son was a little boy."

"We never had a white sofa."

"Are you sure? Think back and try to visualize your living room as it existed then."

"I can see it perfectly. There's no white sofa. We lived in the same house with the same furniture for sixteen years. I would know if we had a white sofa."

"What color was it?"

"Blue."

Could a particular event, object or memory be stored differently in the brains of various people who were witness to it at the same time?

The answer is yes. It turns out that memory is actually a reconstruction of events, feelings and experiences. Once your brain has reconstructed something it's stored in the hippocampus, the part of the brain that's associated with memory, and it gets locked in.

A memory is formed by repeatedly stimulating the same set of nerve cells, which makes the connection between the cells stronger. If we stop thinking about an event or a person the neurons begin to lose their connections and the memory fades or disappears, which is why it's important to preserve good memories by enjoying them over and over again.

Now you know why the scrapbook is in your toolbox. One day your adult child is likely to accuse you of treating him like a baby while he was growing up and embarrassing him by talking about his bad judgment in front of his friends. Resist the urge to defend yourself. Simply take out your scrapbook and show him the pictures taken at his seventh birthday party at which the paramedics had to remove his tongue from a huge block of ice. Be sure to turn the page and point out the photo of the fire department rescuing him from atop an eighty-foot tall tree. You might have to remind him that when he was eight he was sure he could emulate flight by tying elastic bands from the limb of that tree to his waist and taking a mighty leap. Aren't scrapbooks great? You'll all get a big laugh out of it...when he's forty! But I digress...again...so ADD.

Rewind please. It's counterproductive to keep revisiting painful memories of those who've transitioned because doing so results in stronger connections between the neurons, which in turn produces prolonged agony. Therapeutic intervention is an exception because painful memories are examined for the sake of understanding how they impact the present. There's then a greater opportunity to form new, happier memories in the future.

Think you can remember this?

# Creating Good Memories
*my experience*

I was thinking about my Aunt Dot today and I remembered that when I went to visit her she'd always put candies in little dishes on the tables in her apartment. In my little girl's mind she put them out just for me. She invariably had something special cooking or offered me bakery cookies she'd bought for the occasion of my visit. That's how I remember it. I've included this story in my scrapbook so I could introduce her to others, including you, and share what I learned from Aunt Dot.

Thinking of her made me realize that I don't remember a single thing my Aunt Dot ever said to me. Not one. I don't even recall doing anything with her. But I loved her, and I guess that's because of how special I always felt in her presence.

I started thinking of other people I've known. Some have passed and some have just drifted out of my life.

Even when I can't remember much about people I can recall how I felt when I was with them.

As you go through your day remember Aunt Dot and do something to help someone feel special. You'll be remembered for it.

It takes more than a good memory to have good memories.

# Part Four

## Your Mission, Should You Decide To Accept It...

1. Do the nice things you did for your partner when you first fell in love
2. Be a person you can love and respect
3. Be guided by reality rather than blinded by fantasy
4. Assess people according to what they do rather than what they say
5. Take note of what those you love enjoy and do something to show them you remember
6. Be mindful of the ratio of positives to negatives in your relationships and increase the former
7. Honestly portray who you are
8. Share memories of loved ones who've passed by telling their stories
9. Talk to and about those who have passed to keep their spirits alive

# Postscript

You now have the tools to create a joyful life. THE LESSONS AND TOOLS IN THIS BOOK WILL CHANGE YOUR LIFE, BUT ONLY IF YOU USE THEM! I wish I could hug all the people who have the guts to be authentic, because initially, it can be daunting. If this book has given you pause to look honestly at the choices you've made and any discrepancies between who you are now and whom you wish to be, and if you decide to make some changes, I am thrilled beyond words. (Actually, I don't think I've ever been 'beyond words,' but you know what I mean.)

It's my hope that you'll share your stories with me and let me know which tools help you most on your journey. Perhaps you'll find some additional tools along your path and think they might help someone else. If so, please let me know. They could show up in another book. Tools are like quarters; you can never have too many when you're going on a trip. Sometimes the tolls that get us to different places are pretty hefty.

I would be honored to have you visit me when I speak at various venues throughout the country. But if that isn't part of your journey, please visit me on my website and give me your feedback. You can find me at Icanrelatetothat.com.

Remember, it's not about seeing through each other; it's about seeing each other through.

We're all in this together.

With love and best wishes for a successful journey,

Dr. Linda

# Acknowledgements

Every person I've known and countless others whom I've never even met have been contributors to this book. We all affect each other in one way or another.

Some successful breakthrough authors who have earned the love of people throughout the world have had dramatic, positive influences on me. The friendships and respect of people like Jeffrey Wands, Jerry Jampolsky, Diane Cirincianno and Raymond Francis have helped me believe in myself and my abilities. Their encouragement has changed my life. I thank them from the bottom of my heart.

Thank you to my dear friend, Ruth Ann Kalish, who lived in my home for several months during the editing process. Ruth organized my writing, gave me honest feedback and encouragement, and assisted me through the entire process of getting this book out. I came to love, admire and respect Ruth for her brilliant mind and honest approach to life. We have a friendship unlike any I've ever had. What a blessing she continues to be in my life.

Thank you to my incredible soul brother, Joseph Parsons (JP), who was the first person with the "credentials" to embrace me as an artist and creator. His encouragement and praise came at a time when I was ready to change course in my own life journey, and his friendship enabled me to see in myself that which I had not previously been able to accept.

Sly Sharenow, my healing soul sister, has been a constant inspiration to me. She has, by example, set the bar high for integrity and patience. Her positive reaction to my various artistic endeavors has helped me believe I could do whatever I set my mind to doing, and her encouragement has been constant. Sly has shown me what peace looks like when I have forgotten. Thank you to my dear and constant friend.

Thank you also to Broadway's Robert Dragotta, whose praise has been especially meaningful to me because of his experience with successful artists in various genres. I've always felt that if he thought highly of me I must have something special, even if I didn't see it in myself. I treasure his friendship as well as the kindness, sensitivity and love he's shown me over the years.

My gratitude and love go out to Jack Wegh, my brilliant friend and financial advisor without whose sage advice and wisdom I'd probably have risked it all and would now be living in a cardboard box under a streetlight. He never for a moment doubted my abilities. Jack is one of the first people whose praise gave me confidence.

Thank you also to Rich Brooke, my very significant other, who has taught me that deeply loving and trusting someone takes time, and that the pace of love is as slow and steady as it is gratifying and worthwhile.

I want to thank my sweet, loving brother Bob, whose positive comments mean so much to me. Bob brought my attention to aspects of the book that needed tweaking. I'm grateful for his input and kind words, and I'm so proud of him for where he is on his path today.

Thank you to my amazingly strong children, Nikki and Jesse Howard-Bloom. They are my greatest inspiration. They have sustained me in my darkest hours, and their unrelenting encouragement, regardless of the substantial risks I've taken, has shown me the meaning of true acceptance, loyalty and unconditional love. Their permission for me to candidly share their painful histories for the potential benefit of others was both brave and compassionate. They are the heroes of my life and my greatest sources of pride and joy.

Kat Turner, who has been a member of our family and my other daughter since she came to live with us when she was sixteen, deserves a thank you of her own. Watching Kat confront her particular challenges has shown me that regardless of the circumstances, people are as happy as they choose to be. Her strength and beautiful spirit have inspired me to be a more patient, gentle person.

Some of my greatest teachers were the clients I've been privileged to assist over the years. Their faith and trust in me are among the greatest gifts I've ever received, and hardly a day goes by that I don't think of them.

A special thank you goes to some other people whose love and encouragement have been constant over many years and have added to my belief in myself. Among them are Stephanie Howard, Meg Dombeck, Lisha Semester and Peter Schwartz.

I also want to thank the people who've stood by me with understanding and patience during the writing of this book.

Finally, thanks to you dear reader, for your permission to share myself with you and allowing me to assist you in your struggle to find yourself. I am deeply honored.